IT COULD BE WORSE

A MOTIVATIONAL TOUR OF TRAGIC THINGS THAT DID NOT HAPPEN TO YOU.

Nate Ramos

It Could Be Worse

© 2024 Nathan Ramos

ISBN 979-8-35094-201-9

This book is dedicated to: Serotonin imbalance.

Without you I would likely never have been inspired to find ever darker reasons why it ain't so bad after all.

Thank you first and foremost to my wife Rachel, without whose support and encouragement, this book would never have been finished. Thank you also to Jill Cappy for designing the cover and for giving me the chance to start sharing my writing. You gave me the confidence to start this project and gave me my first by-line. Thank you to my mother, Suzi who helped nurture my curiosity and gave me my love of language.

Thank you also to the following people for their financial support for It Could Be Worse:

Adi Noar, Sarah Ramos, Emily Barker, Brent Grantham, Deidra Inman, Julie Reminick, Kelly Ramos, Ron Ramos, Eleanor Cohen, Emily Ramos, Angela Kurzinger, Elizabeth Gerez, Tim Ramos, Jeanette Santiago-Muniz, Bela Mittleman, Liza Adams, Rachel Hildebrandt, Austin Gelhausen, Barbara Drnek, Dave White, Katie White, Samuel Plent, Nicole Wild, Jaclyn Gordon, Joan Drnek, and six anonymous donors.

Introduction

"Life is not about dodging storm clouds;
it is about learning to dance in the rain."

That is a lovely little platitude and might provide just the right amount of positivity to get someone through their day. There is only one problem. That saying is bullshit. "Dancing under storm clouds…" is not a healthy way to deal with adversity, it is a good way to get struck by lightning. You should not "learn to dance in the rain" You should go inside when it is raining.

I'm not sure what is broken in me but whenever I see an inspirational quote like that, I just can't take it seriously. That isn't how the world works and uplifting metaphors just don't grab me. An optimist is always looking at the glass as half full, but there are no half full glasses in a flood. They are all completely full… along with the bowls, the mugs, the basements, and the lungs of the people that drowned in it. "Look at the bright side!" is a fucked-up thing to say to a blind person.

I prefer the opposite approach. When the chips are down, I take comfort in knowing that there are those who have it objectively worse than me. I can shoulder my burdens because they can shoulder theirs. This doesn't solve any problems, but neither does telling someone to, "Open their heart to the world because they never know what they might receive". Opening your heart is instantly fatal and if anything except blood is entering it, you are going to have big problems. If nothing else, I hope this collection lets you know that you are not alone in your pain. The world is suffering with you and thankfully, lots of things have it worse than you.

So, what is this book? It is a motivational guide for people with depression, a dark sense of humor and an appetite for morbid curiosities. What follows is a series of stories of historical events, unlucky lives and unpleasant deaths; there are detailed accounts of human suffering as well as stories of animals whose lives will make you happy you were born a human. You will find no chapters and there are no countdowns. This is a book not a BuzzFeed article. There is no #1 worst thing to be reincarnated as. Suffering, and one's objections to it, are personal. Enjoy the entries and read them however you wish. All I can say is that from beginning to end this book is a carefully and humorously arranged anthology designed to comfort you, to motivate you, to educate you and to hopefully make you laugh. The stories are true, the animals and people are real and so is their pain. If you like your inspiration with a dose of tragedy, a tinge of humor and smattering of trivia, then this book is for you. Enjoy, and remember: It could be worse.

CONTENTS

You Could Be A Pearl Fish

The housing market is a bit of a bitch these days. Depending on where you live, you are either paying a fortune for a shoebox-sized sweat box in a trendy city, or you are trying to figure out if it would be worse to live next to a meth lab just begging to be a crater or in a flood zone with a leaky basement in the midst of a climate crisis.

That is, you dream of actually having the money and credit score to afford either of those options because you are stuck in a vicious lease with nine roommates in a three-bed, two-bath, former frat house with a stripper pole and an open shower in the basement.

A homeless pearlfish (Carapus acus) stares shamefully at the seafloor while looking for shelter. The only thing more degrading than being a homeless pearlfish is living inside someone's ass. Photo: Alessandro Pagano.

Equally likely is that you are in an apartment under what must be a nights-only tap-dancing studio punctuating your day around awkward trips to the community laundry room and equally awkward conversations at the mail slots. None of these scenarios are ideal to say the least, but I am here to tell you that it could have been worse.

You could have been born a **pearlfish.** The name pearlfish is shared by several genera of long, slender, ray-finned fish species of the Carapidae family that live inside the **rectum** of certain **sea cucumbers**. Living inside anything's butt would be a bummer (kill me), but a sea cucumber is an insentient blob that hoovers up sand from the ocean floor like a sex-toy-shaped vacuum cleaner, and you would live in its butt next to an ever-advancing turd made of sand and ocean trash.

Imagine being pushed out of your apartment because the back wall is made of poop-sand, and you and the poop are both being pushed out the front (back) door constantly. Every time the sea cucumber goes #2, you get evicted, and then you must scramble to get back in before another pearlfish beats you to the punch. That's right; the sea cucumber bunghole is actually such a desirable residence for these deviant little sickos that pearlfish have been known to fight to the death over squatting rights to a sea cucumber's butt.

You Could Have a Goddamn Fish Living in Your Ass

You know how you do not have a live fish wriggling around inside your colon? Well, some sea cucumbers do. In case you are wondering why the sea cucumber doesn't just clench and hold whenever the pearlfish starts sniffing around in order to keep it out, there are two reasons:

1. The sea cucumber does not have a brain and thus can't really use the "morning-after-Taco-Bell-with-no-toilet-in-sight" defense of sphincter squeezing and praying.

2. The sea cucumber evolved before some of the finer points of body plans had been worked out. Consequentially, sea cucumbers don't just defecate through their butts, they also breathe through them. This means puckering up to keep out butt-burglars would also mean asphyxiating.

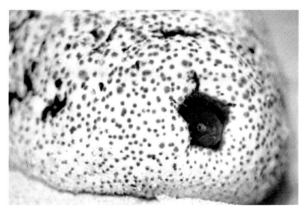

A man (not pictured) photographs a fish sexually assaulting/living in a helpless sea cucumber and does nothing to stop it. Photo by: orangkucing

The poor sea cucumber cannot do anything to keep squatters out of its ass and is powerless to expel the anal intruders once they have moved in.

3

You Could Be Neptune's Exploding Dildo A.K.A. The Sea Cucumber

Even if you do not have a fish fiddling around in your anus, it would suck to be a sea cucumber. We have already mentioned that sea cucumbers never bothered to evolve a brain and that they have a less than modern way of breathing through their nose-butt. More troubling, though, is the sea cucumber's way of protecting itself. Sea cucumbers defend themselves via a process called **auto-evisceration**. This is exactly what it sounds like and involves pushing so hard that the sea cucumber blows its internal organs out its butt in an attempt to distract and/or disgust a would-be predator. Personally, letting my insides get eaten to avoid my outsides getting eaten is sort of a strange tactic, but to each their own. Perhaps **evolution** was too busy trying to figure out how to keep Little **Nemo** and his friends from taking up rooms in the sponge's ass to worry about the little things like how to avoid predation without exploding yourself.

If you were wondering how expelling its organs out of its ass—as one would spray a can of silly string at a fellow partygoer—does not result in the cucumber's death, you are not alone. Sea cucumbers have the ability to regrow basically all of their body tissue, and so disemboweling themselves is a somewhat temporary problem. This rather impressive healing ability does have one major downside, though. The ability to rapidly regrow their tissue means that they have essentially turned themselves into an ever-lasting meatloaf. **Harlequinn crabs** have figured out this helpful life hack whereby they can grab onto the skin of the much larger sea cucumber, eat to their hearts content, wait a few days for the tissue to regenerate, and eat the same piece over and over again. For the crabs it is like an all-you-can-eat buffet, and for the unfortunate cucumber it is an all-you-can-suffer form of medieval torture. Certain species of pearlfish take advantage of this as well. Individuals have been known to eat the gonads and respiratory organs of their hosts. Between their undesirable diet, ass-invading fish, **parasitic** crabs, and exploding lung defense, the sea cucumber is proof that if there is a **god,** he is not all good.

*Two of the main flavors of sea cucumber: alien sex toy, and poop rolled in sand. Not pictured are the **free-swimming penis impersonators** and flesh covered feather dusters. Photo: François Michonneau, Bernard DUPONT*

You Could Be Turned Into A Zombie And Eaten Alive

Nobody wants to be a **cockroach**. Sure, you could be notoriously hardy and adaptable, but that resiliency comes at a cost. For one, being hard to kill would make answering the call of the void quite difficult as you could not off yourself by decapitation, desiccation, elemental exposure, radiation **poisoning**, or any number of other readily available suicide means. Now, you may think that not being able to kill yourself is a good thing, but you wouldn't if you had a predator like the **emerald jewel wasp** (Ampulex compressa).

This horror-show sicko paralyzes its victims with a sting to the belly, then delivers another surgically precise sting to the roach's brain. This placates and possibly controls the actions of the now helpless insect. Now that the roach has been zombified, the wasp bites off an antenna and drinks some of the cockroach's blood (seems unnecessarily cruel, but okay) before pulling her victim along by the leg/leash. The brain-dead but **ambulatory** bug is guided to a hidey-hole where the momma jewel wasp lays an egg in the still very alive cockroach. A few days later, the jewel wasp larva hatches and consumes the roach from the inside.

From the moment that the roach is stung, it is completely incapable of escaping or fighting back. The entire horrific encounter is like one of those nightmares where you can never punch back or run, but instead of waking up at the end, you just kind of sit in a dark hole and wait for a baby wasp to eat you to death.

Emerald jewel wasp (top) whispers flirtatiously to cockroach (paralyzed, bottom). "How would you like to come back to my place and let my child eat you alive from the inside out?" The cockroach attempts to scream but can't because God gave it resistance to radiation instead of vocal chords. Photo: Dianakc

You Could Give Birth Through Your Penis (Sort Of)

Such is the life of the female **spotted hyena**. Yes, I said female. Let me explain. Life on the Savannah is hard, and it pays to be tough. So much so that evolution decided to start juicing some of the inhabitants to help them bulk up a little. Hyena culture is **matriarchal**, which means the ladies run the show. Female hyenas have to fight over their share of a kill, and to help boost the aggression needed for constant social jockeying, they've evolved to produce a lot of extra **testosterone**. These ladies have so much extra T that their genitals have gotten a little confused.

Spotted hyenas (Crocuta crocuta) sharing a carcass. The second individual from the left has something between her legs, and it is not a tail or a wiener.
Credit: Thomas Fuhrmann

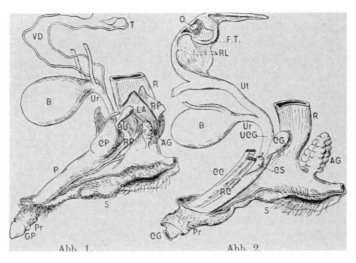

One of these confusing-ass drawings of hyena genitals is that of a male; the other drawing depicts those of a female. The fact that it is not immediately clear which is which is why giving birth to a hyena pup would suck balls. Illustration from: Anatomischer Anzeiger c.1922

These confused genitals still function but they look rather… masculine. The hyena **vagina** opens into a long tube formed out of her highly modified **clitoris**. This organ is so phallic-looking that scientists call it a **pseudo-penis**. It can be eight inches long and even become erect.

So yeah, it's pretty weird that the female hyenas kind of have wieners but gender bending is cooler than it has ever been, so that isn't really the problem. The problem is that female hyenas must still give birth through that vagina, and by necessity, also then through the fake **skin-flute**. So brutal is this birth via dick-hole arrangement that one third of first-time mothers die from the resulting bleeding. The two thirds that do survive wish that they hadn't because of the tearing. That's right, tearing. It is not uncommon for the pseudo-penis to become more of a pseudo-ribbon during this rather excruciating delivery, and very often it never heals.

Imagine if instead of your mother taking you to get circumcised as a baby, you were the one who circumcised your mother. Instead of a trim around the top, it is more of a permanent down the middle part.

You Could Be Trapped Inside Your Mother's Penis (Sort Of)

You see, the pseudo-penis thing doesn't just make childbirth a bitch for the mom. Sixty percent of first- born hyena cubs die in their mother's confusing-ass birth canal. Death comes either from suffocation while stuck mid-shaft or from bleeding to death because the cub's umbilical cord is not long enough to stretch from the womb to the tip of the she-nis.

BABY HECTOR
THE HYENA
JUN 8, 2023
JUN 8, 2023

CHOKED ON MOTHER'S FORESKIN, NO, NOT LIKE THAT...

An all too familiar headstone in the hyena community. R.I.P. sweet prince…
Gone but not forgotten. Photo credit: Chris Eason

You Could Be A Victim Of Predatory Testicular Violence

I'm telling you, you do not want to be anything with **testicles** (real ones) that live where spotted hyenas live. I was feeling pretty bad for hyenas until I learned that hyenas like to employ a very brutal hunting technique The animals that hyenas hunt had to evolve alongside lions, cheetahs, leopards, wild dogs and well... ...hyenas. With neighbors like that, African game animals developed lots of horns and teeth and other stabby appendages that makes frontal attacks quite risky. As such, hyenas prefer to bring down large prey by clamping their jaws onto the ball sacks of hapless **quadrupeds** and holding on until the target's **scrote** tears off and the poor thing bleeds to death. Actually, after watching hours of incredibly uncomfortable hyena hunts, it is painfully clear that hyenas don't really bother to wait for their mutilated prey to actually die before eating them. They just start munching away while the poor thing bellows and cries and the first thing dangling out of the hyena's mouth is often the animal's genitals.

Part of me thinks that hyenas just want the rest of the animal kingdom to feel as much genital agony as they are forced to and part of me thinks that there is simply a serious, ungodly disregard for anything resembling male sex organs in the African Savannah.

This cape buffalo (left) is about to die in just the worst fucking way.
Credit: Youtube; The wild Animal Kingdom

You Could Have Been The World's Unluckiest Astronomer

You could have had the luck of the late Guillaume Hyacinthe Jean-Baptiste Le Gentil de la Galasaisiere.

"Gentil" as he will be called from now on because-Jesus-Christ-look-at-his-goddamn-name-I'm-not-typing-that-again was part of a project to accurately measure the distance from the **Earth** to the **Sun**. The idea was to observe the **transit of Venus** across the Sun's face and compare measurements on time and distance with hundreds of other scientists watching the phenomenon from around the world.

Gentil set out for **Pondicherry**, India in 1760 to witness the transit but things got fucky pretty much right from jump street. His ship was blown off course, war broke out, the observatory was captured, and eventually Gentil's ship was forced to abandon the voyage and return to France. The day of the transit came, and Venus passed in front of the Sun while Gentil was at sea where the rolling waves and obnoxious sea shanties made astronomical measurements impossible.

Guillaume Hyacinthe Jean-Baptiste Le Gentil de la Galasaisiere Longest Name Ever (pictured left) exudes the fiery personality and raw sex appeal for which his profession is known, while posing for a portrait in between not seeing Venus once and not seeing Venus twice.

Undeterred, Gentil decided to stay to witness the next transit which was conveniently due in only eight short years. Gentil spent the intervening years dealing with bouts of **dysentery,** more war, strife, sabotage, **cholera** and general setbacks until at last the day came… and alas… the sky was overcast. The transit occurred while no observations were possible. Ten years of waiting were lost to a single cloud. According to records, the skies were overcast all morning and cleared moments after Venus was no longer visible. "No big deal," said a heartbroken Gentil. He could wait for the next transit easy-peasy. Except he couldn't really since he was already forty-four and the next transit wouldn't be for another 121 years.

A defeated Gentil returned home to find that he had been declared dead, his wife had remarried, his position at the royal academy had been given away and his relatives had divided and squandered his estate. Oh well, that is what you get for going into a **S.T.E.M.** field, nerd. It turns out that even if Gentil had recorded the transit of Venus, the measurements obtained by the other scientists were so inconsistent that the project was scrapped. So even if he had succeeded, he would have lost everything only to have his findings disregarded.

In summary, Gentil traveled halfway around the world, survived wars, disease, and monsoons, spent ten years of his life devoted to a project he would never actually participate in, lost his title, his job, his home, his wife and everything he owned. In the end, it was all for nothing. So, the next time you feel disappointed because a project you started gets scrapped or you catch hell from the missus for working late, just be glad you didn't spend over a decade in the **malaria**-rich, sweaty part of the world working on a job that ruined your entire life.

You Could Have Been The World's Unluckiest Astronomer's Wife

You could have been Le Gentil's wife. Yeah, we kind of skipped right over the fact that the world's unluckiest astronomer had a spouse. I have a hard enough time convincing my wife to let me go fishing for a couple of hours, but somehow this guy cleared a two-year long guys trip to India and she was like "Okay, that's fine babe, but if I don't hear from you in ten years, I'm selling everything and leaving you." Gentil probably laughed and said, "Ahh sweety, I love you and your sassy humor," and he kissed her good-bye before fucking off to Pondicherry. Little did he know that Mrs. Gentil wasn't being funny.

When I read about this story I was like, you left your wife and job and said, "I'll see you in two years," and then decided, "Ehh... two years... eleven years... they'll understand?" Certainly, you can't just give yourself eight extra years of vacation time and not tell your boss and wife and expect everybody to be cool with it.

I know that. You know that. And as it turns out, Gentil knew that. Gentil actually wrote hundreds of letters explaining his intentions and detailing his scientific exploits in the years he spent abroad. The problem was that war and the general shittiness of international postal services at the time meant that none of his letters made it to their destination. But this entry isn't about Gentil so forget him. We are talking about his wife. Can you imagine your husband leaving you for a 720 day long weekend and then not texting you a single time during that stretch?

"Oh, you were looking through your crusty little telescope the whole day huh? No time to write a postcard? Not five minutes?" I do not know how long it took for Gentil to be presumed legally dead* but I'm guessing he was dead to his wife a long time before that. Imagine wondering for years what happened to your husband, finally coming to grips with his death, losing everything and moving on and then your delinquent husband comes back with literally nothing to show for his absence except some stories about nearly shitting himself to death with dysentery.

*Being declared "**dead in absentia**" is a legal status that can be granted when no one has heard from you in an extended period of time and you are not expected to be alive, such as when a plane crashes or a boat is lost at sea and no bodies are recovered. This can even be done without direct evidence of your death, or when you piss off your wife enough that she tells everyone you died.*

You Could Have Been A Living Breathing Smoldering Metaphor For Bad Luck

You could have been **Roy Sullivan**. Roy Sullivan was a national park ranger who worked in Shenandoah National Park for thirty-five years. Mr. Sullivan currently holds the record for having survived the most lightning strikes of any person. He was struck a total of seven times in his life between 1942 to 1977. The odds of being struck by lightning seven non-consecutive times has been calculated at one in 10^28 power if you speak nerd, or one in 10,000,000,000,000,000,000,000,000,000 if you prefer your numbers with an unsayable amount of zeros behind them.

That is to say that Roy had truly unimaginable bad luck. What's even more truly unimaginable is that a grown man who had been struck by lightning before apparently never learned what a goddamn thundercloud looks like and then never learned that again six more times.

Roy "Smokey the Ear" Sullivan poses in uniform, holding evidence of his lack of situational awareness. Credit: National Park Service

Timeline Of Roy Sullivan's Life:

- Feb. 7, 1912- Roy is born (presumably under a ladder surrounded by black cats while his mother smashed every mirror in sight.)

- April 1942- Roy is struck by lightning while escaping a burning building. (Which was set alight because it had also been struck.)

- July 1969- Roy is somehow struck by lightning through his truck window.

- July 1970- Roy is struck in his front yard after insulting a passing light-ning bolt (I made that last part up fact checkers, now what?)

- 1972- Roy is somehow struck while inside a ranger station which at this point it is kind of like... this is like a very drawn-out **Final Destination** movie with just one kind of death sequence.

- August 1973- Roy is struck after driving away from a storm. He supposedly thought he was far enough away and got out of the truck where he was promptly struck. (Why a man who had already been struck by lightning five fucking times would ever trust himself to judge what is, and what is not, a safe distance to be from a thunder-storm is beyond me.)

- June 1976- Roy apparently tried to outrun a storm and surprise, surprise, the superheated bolt of electrical energy that can travel the speed of light caught up to him.

- June 1977- Roy was fishing on an overcast day when to the shock of absolutely no one (but Roy) he was struck by lightning via the giant conductive pole in his hands for the seventh and final time.

You Could Have Been The Beneficiary Of Roy Sullivan's Will

I cannot help but imagine Mrs. Human Lightning Rod sitting there, waiting for a payday that seemed inevitable given her husband's propensity for conducting electricity. I can see her at the kitchen table, muttering to herself, "Any day now old man lightning rod with his cosmically bad luck and piss poor decision making is going to get lit up, and I will be getting me that sweet, sweet park service pension check."

Time and time again, the crazy coot saunters inside with his blackened head still smoldering saying, "Yur not gonna believe this honey..." Your only consolation would be that Roy just can't help but watch a good gully-washer from one of those mountain tops, open fields, bare hills and lone **trees** that literally everyone else avoids when there is thunder. Maybe, just maybe, next time will be your lucky day... but it won't.

Why not? Because Roy finally did what an estimated seven billion volts of electricity administered over three decades could not. Roy took his own life, shooting himself in 1983 and almost certainly voiding any life insurance policy. If you are thinking to yourself; "Well that isn't funny that's just super dark and depressing," then you are right. It is tragic. What story about getting hunted by the forces of nature and living in fear of the heavens has a happy ending? This isn't a Disney movie, it is the messed up **German** fairytale they are based on. Except it isn't a fairy tale, it happened.

You Could Have Been A German Child Growing Up When All The Nursery Rhymes Were Horror Stories

Remember when you were little, and all your bed-time stories were about murder, **rape**, evil parents, deception, and **cannibalism?** Yeah, me neither. Most parents seem to think that scaring the ever-living hell out of their kids is not a good strategy for a good night's sleep. That was not always the case. The origin stories for your favorite Disney movies were pretty gory and more than a little fucked up.

These tales of terror would have been lost to the sands of time were it not for two German brothers named Wilhelm and Jacob Grimm. **The Brothers Grimm** collected and published a disturbing anthology of folk-tales, many of which were aimed at children.

Let us explore a few of the batshit crazy stories that German peasants used to scar their little mini-mensches.

Snow White: Snow White wasn't originally hunted by her stepmom; she was poisoned by her actual mom. In the original story, Snow White's mom is a queen who kills her husband and hates her daughter for being more beautiful than her which is a totally acceptable reason to want to kill your daughter. I mean, who hasn't asked a magic mirror if their children are hotter than them and then killed that child because the answer was "yes"? Oh yeah, no one has ever done that because that is an absurd opening to a children's story.

Because of what follows, it is worth noting that Snow White is seven years old at this point in the story. Snow White's mom hires a hitman (the huntsman) who is ordered to kill Snow White and return with her lungs and liver as proof that the deed has been done. The Huntsman says, "Okay, nothing weird about that request" and goes in search of his prey. He drags Snow White into the woods but has a change of heart because he is taken by her beauty. I cannot overstate that this dude was fine with killing a second grader before he found out she was pretty. Anyways, the merciful but incredibly shallow Huntsman lets her go. And by "go," I mean he just fucking abandons her in the wilderness, which I personally feel is the same thing as killing her but that's irrelevant.

Meanwhile, the queen is sitting there waiting for her daughter's guts to show up, and in walks the huntsman with a soggy bag of body parts. How exactly the queen planned on recognizing her daughter's organs as genuine is not explained. The huntsman presents the queen with pig's entrails. Still thinking that they are Snow White's, the queen eats them... like you do. When the world's snitchiest magic mirror tells the queen that her daughter isn't dead the queen is all like "What?! You mean I ate pork instead of my daughter?! Goddammit!" The queen finds Snow White shacked up with the seven dwarves and tries to kill her twice before settling on poisoning an apple and just sort of handing it to her. Why Snow White accepted fruit from someone that had just tried to kill her multiple times is also not explained. Once Snow White is dead the queen just leaves and years pass while Snow White's corpse is just sitting in an open casket in the woods. A prince who is just ambling through the woods sees Snow White for the first time and begs the dwarves to let him take a random-ass dead kid back to his castle. The dwarves feel bad for him and let him take Snow White's dead, seven-year-old body away to do God knows what with.

That may seem extremely weird but I'm sure the prince had nothing perverted in mind. Just your standard guy finds a child's corpse in the woods and wants to take her home with him because she is pretty scenario. One of the servants being employed to haul the casket back to the prince's castle gets angry at the little dead girl for being so heavy and fucking slaps her. (Yeah, a child's pallbearer slapped her corpse, you read that right.) Doing so knocks the poisoned apple out of her mouth and she wakes up and marries the prince, which is not odd. The queen/evil witch/bride's mom attends their wedding but is outed as Snow White's would-be murderer and arrested. The prince makes his new mother-in-law wear red-hot iron shoes until she dances herself to death. So at least there is a happy ending. For the audience, not for Snow White. She becomes a child-bride and an orphan on the same day. The most memorable moment from her wedding is when her homicidal mother gets tortured to death at the reception.

Rendering of the prince looking over a seven-year-old's corpse and contemplating how weird it would be if he asked these little people if he can just, you know, take her body and totally not commit crimes against nature with it.
Illustration by Alexander Zick

Attempted child murder, attempted cannibalism, attempted statutory rape (I mean the prince probably waited eleven years to consummate the marriage, right?) and torture. I'd make that into the first ever feature length animated movie, wouldn't you? Believe it or not, this is actually one of the tamer stories.

Sleeping Beauty: Sleeping Beauty is less about true love's kiss and more about infidelity and rape. A random king is strolling by the castle that Sleeping Beauty is power napping in when his falcon flies into her window. He breaks down the door and upon seeing a beautiful woman who cannot be awakened he decides to bang her and then leave. She gives birth to twins who suckle at her fingers and in doing so remove the poisoned fiber that put her under. (In the original it is a piece of flax not a spindle that pricks her finger.) Speaking of pricks, the King decides he wants another "visit" and is very surprised to learn that his living sex doll is awake and nursing twins. The King tells Sleeping Beauty that he loves her, which is apparently an acceptable explanation for date rape because she returns with him to his kingdom. The King's wife is there, and she is not super happy to see Sleeping Beauty or her bastard children. She takes it pretty well all things considered. She asks the royal cook to kill the kids and cook them for her faithless husband. The cook decides not to and instead serves lamb. The King finds out and, orders the cook to kill and cook the queen instead and he does. Sleeping Beauty, her children and the creepy-ass King eat the queen and live happily ever after while the cook attends medieval therapy.

Cinderella: Grimm's version of **Cinderella** is largely familiar except for a few key details. Cinderella doesn't have a fairy godmother. She prays to a tree that was planted over her mother's grave, and it grows dresses for her to wear. You know, like trees do. There are multiple dresses because there were originally three royal balls that Cinderella attends. She dances with the prince on all three occasions but always leaves before the ball is over which is not explained. At the final ball, the prince covers the stairs with sticky pitch so that she cannot escape. It doesn't work as intended though because she simply slips out of the glass slipper when it becomes glued to the steps.

Apparently, the man could conceive of booby trapping his front porch but not asking his crush for her for goddamn name.

Once he starts touring the country with the glass slipper the evil **stepsisters** show up. Except in the original, they don't just fail to put on the glass slipper- they chop off their toe and heel respectively in order to try to make it work. Two talking birds rat the sisters out because I guess the prince didn't see the blood pooling inside of the transparent glass shoe. We are talking about a man who fell madly in love with someone whose face he could not pick out of a line up after 3 dates.

Cinderella then gets to try on the slipper that has her evil stepsisters' blood all over it and the prince carries her off to be married. The evil stepsisters get their eyes gouged out at the wedding and you have another happy ending.

There are some folk stories that were too dark for even the House of Mouse to try to adapt. Stories such as these:

The Juniper Tree: A rare non-homicidal mother makes a brief appearance before dying while giving birth to her son. Her husband buries her beneath a **juniper tree** and remarries. That marriage produces a daughter. Wife number two sets about abusing her stepson because apparently stepmoms are always evil. The evil stepmom lures the boy with the promise of an apple that is in the bottom of a deep chest. When he leans in to grab it, she slams the door shut and fucking decapitates him. Then she maniacally gets her own daughter to believe that she's killed him by propping the boy's head onto his body and encouraging the girl to push him. When his head falls off, his sister understandably loses her shit and evil mom tells the girl that if she says nothing about the "accident" to her father then she won't get in trouble. Evil stepmom (I feel like I can just say stepmom at this point, since they are all evil in these stories) chops the boy up and makes a "blood porridge" out of him. She then serves him to his dad for supper. I'm not sure what is more fucked up about that; the fact that the stepmother served a man his own child for supper or that European peasants used to eat something called "blood porridge".

Original artwork of The Juniper Tree from "Household Stories" by The Brothers' Grimm. Nothing shouts domestic life quite like murdering your child and blaming it on your other child. Also you will note that the story was originally called "The Almond Tree" but it was changed because junipers are objectively more magical than almonds... probably. Illustration by Walter Crain

The deeply scarred daughter buries her half-brother's bones under the juniper tree next to his mom, and a bird appears. The bird is the reincarnated spirit of the boy, who promptly flies around town singing a song about what his stepmother did to him. The townsfolk respond as any rationally thinking person might and promptly turn the stepmother over to the authorities. Just kidding, instead they give the bird a gold chain, a pair of shoes and a millstone… …like you do. The bird/boy gives his dad the chain, his sister the shoes and drops the millstone on his murderous stepmom's head which kills her. Successful revenge is apparently the recipe for resurrection because the boy is transformed back into a human and everyone lives happily ever after… …except for the traumatized daughter who saw her brother's head roll off before a bird smashed her mother's brains in with a rock.

The Robber Bridegroom: A **miller** is approached by a wealthy suitor who wishes to marry his daughter. The miller agrees and the two are engaged. The newly affianced suitor complains that his soon-to-be bride has not visited him and sends for her. She follows a trail of ashes to his house which is apparently the 1600s' version of **MapQuest.** When the girl arrives, a bird tells her to leave, a message which she ignores (stupid), and then an old woman appears and also tells her to leave. The old woman discloses that the girl's fiancé is actually a murderous cannibal, but before they can do anything the man shows up. The old woman hides the girl in an empty wine cask before opening the door. The bridegroom enters with a band of ruffians who have abducted another girl. They strip the girl, violate her and then chop her to pieces. (Why on earth you would invite your fiancée to your place and then immediately bring your boys over for a gang rape/cannibalism session is beyond me.) During the unmentionable activities that I just mentioned, one of the girl's fingers is chopped off and flies into the empty wine cask. The old woman (whose presence at the murder house is never explained) convinces the men not to look for the finger and drugs their wine. Once they have passed out both women flee. (I'm not sure why the old woman didn't do that before the bride showed up but whatever.) The wedding takes place not long after, and our bride waits until the wedding feast to produce the finger of the murdered girl. She recounts the entire story, which prompts the groom and his gang to be put to death. Hopefully she had the decency to wait until after dinner service was finished because I'm assuming the party is over after a confession like that, and some of those guests probably came from quite a ways off. Alas, the Grimm Brothers do not say one way or another in their retelling.

I think the most important thing to take away from all these stories is that they are not parables, and no moral is presented at the end of the tale. It is just story after story of the most terrible, and nonsensical things happening to people who mostly don't deserve it, and then you put your whimpering kids to sleep with no lesson or wisdom to take away and that's the end of it. In an age of high mortality, unregulated child labor, and general squalor, not even the bedtimes stories were enjoyable. My God the past was terrible!

You Could Have Been Fighting A War That Ended Thirty Years Ago

When I say that, I don't mean the poor bastards suffering from PTSD and reliving the unspeakable things they were forced to do in the name of spreading **democracy** and **McDonald's** franchises. I'm speaking about the insane story of **Hiroo Onoda.**

Hiroo was a Japanese intelligence officer stationed on a small island in the **Philippines** during **WWII**. Hiroo was the prototypical Japanese soldier, fanatically loyal to his country and fiercely devoted to the war cause. He and his comrades believed that certain pamphlets dropped on his position by American planes in September of 1945 were a trick meant to draw them out of hiding. They were not. The pamphlets were genuinely meant to inform them of **Japan's** unconditional surrender. Because Hiroo thought his country would never consider surrender under any circumstances, he ignored the news. Hiroo remained tucked away in a mountain enclave, fighting, raiding, and refusing to surrender for twenty-nine years after WWII officially ended.

He and his small unit led a guerilla war on the nearby villages until all but Hiroo were killed by police or had deserted. For three decades they stole provisions, carried out raids and killed as many as thirty locals. Eventually only Hiroo was left, but he continued to fight until someone tracked down his former commanding officer and brought him to the island to try to convince Hiroo to "cut the shit". This officer formally ordered Hiroo to lay down his arms and surrender and Hiroo finally complied.

Because of Hiroo's actions he became the last Japanese soldier to surrender, doing so in 1974. Hiroo lived in hiding for twenty-nine years, living off the land, masturbating with no **porn,** stealing pigs from locals, and occasionally shooting at people for no reason other than his mistaken belief that he was still a combatant. Imagine the kind of "seriously, my bad guys..." type of apology you must have to give after terrifying a village for almost thirty years because no one told you to stop. That is, no one that *you believed* told you to stop. Like soooo many people tried to tell him that he could stop killing villagers and stealing their stuff because he was "at war".

Hiroo Onoda (pictured right) gifts his officer's sword to Philippine President Ferdinand Marcos (left) upon his official surrender. Everybody seems pretty chill considering that Hiroo merc'ed dozens of civilians AFTER the war ended but hey, he didn't know so... ...no harm, no foul right? Photo: Philippine Government

You Could Have The Worst Neighbor Ever

You could have been Hiroo Onoda's neighbors between 1945 and 1974. I have heard about some pretty shitty **homeowners' associations** and we all know a Karen whose voice makes you want to throw grenades at them. However, that is not the same as having actual grenades thrown at you by your neighbor every time he runs out of chickens, which incidentally, he stole from you last time he was "on patrol". Imagine waking up, going to grab the mail, and hearing someone scream "Banzai!!!!!" while charging you with a samurai sword, thereby forcing you and the rest of the block to take up defensive positions all before your morning coffee. Imagine that, and then imagine that this happens for twenty-nine goddamned years.

Pictured above: The kind of bullshit the average citizen of Lubang Island could expect to see coming at them when they were walking their dogs, feeding the chickens or playing catch with the kiddos from 1945-1974

You Could Have Been
Hit By A Rock... ...From Space

Such is the case of **Ann Elizabeth Hodges.** On November 30, 1954, Ann was resting peacefully in her **Alabama** home when she was struck by an 8.5-pound **meteorite** that had just crashed through her roof, going approximately 120 mph. Ann survived the violent strike and remains the only human to ever be unlucky enough to have been hit by a meteorite. The chances of that happening have been likened to simultaneously being in a tornado, and inside a hurricane while being struck by lightning. On top of all of this, this meteorite strike happened while Ann was napping, which means not only was she hit by a friggin' space rock, but she was also woken up from a nap in possibly the rudest way imaginable.

That was not the only rude awakening she was in for, though. The meteorite was confiscated by the **US government**, who feared the rock may have been a piece of Soviet tech or piece of a failed missile launch. Ann had hoped to cash in on the valuable space rock to cover the cost of replacing her roof and covering her medical bills. When the Feds concluded that the meteorite was in fact just a useless, priceless space rock and not Soviet spy gear, they eventually returned it. Ann's custody battle over the rock that tried to smush her took another turn. Her landlord also thought the meteorite was valuable and claimed that because it fell on his property, he should be the proper owner. Ann had to go to court and eventually settled with her landlord for the price of $500. That means that Ann had to effectively buy the rock that nearly killed her for the equivalent of $5,500 in 2023 money.

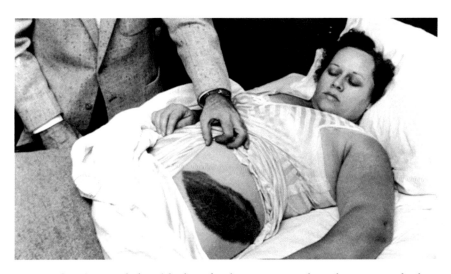

Ann Hodges (pictured above) looking for the exact spot where the meteorite hit her. Her best guess was that it was somewhere near the massive swollen bruise on her side Credit: Jay Leviton

You Could Have Been The Unluckiest Meteor In The Cosmos

You could have been a meteor that was ejected from a faraway, primordial explosion that travelled across the vast cosmos, enduring the unfathomable expanse of the **universe**; witnessing grand, indescribable events; and spiraling through the chasms of endless endlessness for billions of years just to finally land in freaking Alabama.

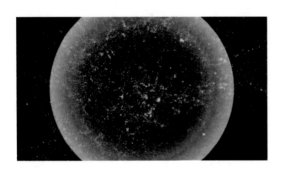 

(On the left) The known universe. A place filled with an inconceivable, near infinite number of possible destinations spread out across the uncountable expanse of literally everything in existence.

(On the right) The state in which you are most likely to be stabbed to death by a man wearing nothing but denim overalls and a toothless smile. A.K.A. not where a meteor wants to end its intergalactic journey.

You Could Be From Alabama

That's it, you could be from Alabama*. That's it. That is the whole joke.

*I would be worried about alienating an entire state's population if not for two reasons.

    1. Only ¾ of adult Alabamians can actually read (76.1%)

    2. If they got this far, they already bought the book so fuck 'em.

You Could Have Been The Only Person In Town Who Didn't Win The Lottery

You could have been the only person in your town who didn't win the **lottery**. When a local women's group distributed what would turn out to be winning lottery tickets to everyone in the town of Sodeto, **Spain**, as part of a fundraiser, they accidentally forgot one resident. A **Greek** filmmaker named **Costis Mitsotakis** instantly became the poorest and saltiest* resident of Sodeto while his neighbors- all of them -split a 950-million-dollar jackpot. Can you imagine that conversation?

Costis: "Mornin' neighbor! Say, what's all the ruckus over at Jerry's?"

Neighbor: "Oh, they are just celebrating his lottery win. You know, deciding what to do with the winnings."

Costis: "Oh, Jerry won?! No way! That's awesome! Good for him!"

Neighbor: "Who cares about Jerry? I'm trying to figure out what to do with mine!"

Costis: "You won too?! That's unbelievable! Congratulations!"

Neighbor: "What are you talking about, Costis? We all won!"

Costis: "That's really sweet of you, man, thinking of your whole family in all this. That's a really good outlook."

Neighbor: "No, I mean we all did. Everybody."

Costis: "Well, clearly not everybody. How's that possible?"

Neighbor: "The whole town did! Check your ticket, man. You know, the ticket we were all given without anyone being left out. I mean, how lucky are we to not only have the winning number but to also have such a wholesome and thoughtful town committee who included every single person in their thoughtless act so that in the incredibly small chance that we won, we could all share in the profit! I mean, we can afford anything now. Every single driveway will have a Ferrari and every house will be filled with riches. A whole town of only millionaires! It's crazy! …Costis, buddy you're looking a little pale, you feeling alright?"

*Actually, if you believe his New York Times interview about the event, he wasn't actually salty about it but that's bullshit right?

You Could Have Had To Listen To The Only Guy Who Didn't Win The Lottery Constantly Bitch About it

You could have been any of the newly minted millionaires trying to enjoy a life of ease in Sodeto whenever they talked about spending any of their new wealth in front of old Costis. Sure they felt bad for the only poor guy in town, but it wasn't their fault he was forgotten about. They were just trying to live off their good fortune without being guilt-tripped about everything. But of course, they were going to hear, "Must be nice" grumbled under Costis's breath every single time someone spent a single frivolous dollar.

You Could Be A Parasitic Sperm Bank

That is to say you could be a male **anglerfish**. Anglerfish live in the deep ocean, far beyond the level that sunlight can penetrate. The only light there is produced by **bioluminescent** animals who use their glowing, flashing and pulsing body parts to aid in all kinds of things. Some critters use their literal flesh lights to help attract prey, while others use them to find a mate and still others, to confuse or distract predators. The anglerfish is in the first camp and dangles a fleshy glowing bit down in front of its long needle-like teeth in hopes that a very stupid fish will come investigate. Male anglerfish are prone to meet the same sticky end as their prey, because they rely in part on following the light signals given off by female anglerfish in order to find them. This leads to some instances of male anglers laying down their best pick-up lines to a bioluminescent eel that promptly eats them.

Imagine dating by going down your street and knocking on everyone's door whenever they turn their kitchen light on. When they answer the door, there are three possibilities. 1) they are food, and you get to eat. 2) They are a female angler, and you get to bone. 3) It was a trap, and something bigger and nastier than you violently tears you apart.

Okay, so the male angler blindly wanders around tapping on anything that blips until he gets laid or fed or dies, and he somehow manage to do the first one. Repeating that same rigamarole year after year is a nightmare, so he decides to just stick with the female angler fish once he finds her. The angler elects to take that very literally and bites down on the female's ass and doesn't let go.

Instead of slapping him, the female just kind of keeps swimming. She ignores him and he keeps biting. It is sort of anticlimactic in several senses of the word. Something is happening though. Over the coming weeks the male will lose his eyes, fins, and most of his organs as he transforms into a fully parasitic nutsack with thoughts. He will live off his wife's blood supply and take in nutrients as needed. His only job now is to provide sperm when required and not fight the other testicles with gills/husbands. That's right; he will likely not be the only male permanently fused to his wife's ass. She may have as many as three pairs of sentient gonads by the time she is done collecting mates.

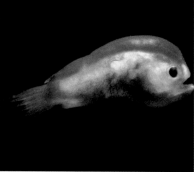

The terrifying, nightmare-inducing little demon on the left is a female anglerfish, the translucent snot-rocket with fins on the right is a male anglerfish. Photos: D. Shale

You Could Be Literally Stuck With The Most Useless Baby-Daddy

You could be a female anglerfish who lives in the same terrifying abyssal blackness as everybody else, playing the world's shittiest game of hide and seek, but you are literally stuck for life with the first asshole who sneaks up on you and latches onto your belly.

Any ladies in the audience thinking that men are basically **parasites** anyway and surmising that having a built-in sex toy that can't ruin dates by **mansplaining** things to them doesn't sound so bad should keep in mind the **sex** is going to be pretty underwhelming. More specifically, it isn't going to happen. Once the male is done fusing to the female's body, semen is transferred directly into the female's body at the site of attachment, and fertilization happens without any need for anything fun. The female has no control over this process, and nothing remotely pleasurable take place. Whereas a human female who is underwhelmed by her partner's sexual performance can just "take matters into her own hands," keep in mind that fish have no hands and no access to **vibrators**.

Two male anglerfish (pictured left) attached to the ventral side of the much larger female (right). Note the male on the top is further along in the whole "dissolving into a nutsack with fins" thing. This is what passes for an anglerfish threesome. No consent, no foreplay, and the only penetration happening is teeth. Kinky? Yes. Pleasurable? Certainly not.

You Could Have Your Dick Destroyed By A Spider Bite

You could be one of about 4000 people who are bitten by **Brazilian wandering spiders** (*Phoneutria nigriventer*) each year. Getting bitten by a spider sucks no matter what (unless you are Peter Parker), but if you happen to be a man who gets a tooth-tickle from the wandering spider, you will likely end up with an involuntary, painful and long-lasting erection which must be surgically deflated. If you're assuming that the bite must be incredibly arousing or sexually pleasing to the victim in order to have that effect, you would be wrong. It is a fucking spider bite. It hurts like hell and causes swelling, sweats, cramping, tissue death, and for some reason, a spike in the chemicals that tell the **penis** that it's showtime… …oh, and sometimes death. So, imagine getting bitten by a massive spider, managing to make it to the hospital, being given the antidote to the **venom** and thinking you are out of the woods and then all the sudden the doctor says, "Not so fast Miguel! We need to stab a turkey baster into your penis and deflate it or the lack of circulation will cause it to fall off."

You would be left telling your buddies the worst possible story about getting your dick sucked.

A wandering spider contemplates whether or not it is the strangest thing to ever give a human an erection. Photo: Dick Culbert

You Could Have Spider Venom Tested On You To Make Better Boner Pills Maybe

How would you like to have spider venom injected into your penis in the name of science? Most of us would say no to this alarming proposal; a disturbing percentage of respondents would probably ask, "For how much?"; and the rest would be running for cover.

Unfortunately, there are just too many ways in which putting actual poison into human genitals can go wrong, and so if new drugs are to be developed, we must turn to animal test subjects in order to work out the kinks. For this reason, and for countless others, be thankful that you are not one of the most truly unfortunate beasts known as the **laboratory rat.**

You could be one of the lab rats that are actually being used right now to study the efficacy of wandering spider venom as a natural alternative to Viagra. The poor wretches are injected with components of the venom, and then a needle is pushed into their little rat boners to measure if there is a pressure change. The rats endure this all so that impotent humans can have sex a few more times. (Not exactly as noble a cause as curing Alzheimer's or bone cancer). Also, I can only assume the job of rat-dick-needle-inserter belongs to an **unpaid intern,** which means that a disgruntled, hung-over college kid is going to be doing the poking.

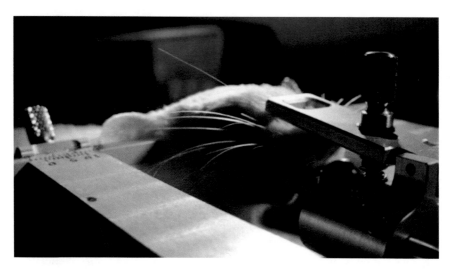

This laboratory rat is part of an important experiment to see how hard you can screw this doo-hickey down before the rat dies. Crucial research such as this is helping to unlock the secrets of the universe and improve the lives of everyone on Earth... ... well, everyone except for the lab rats. Photo: Sheila J. Toro

You Could Be Measuring Rat Erections For School Credit

You could be an unpaid intern whose life dream was to travel to the Amazon and contribute to our understanding of one of the most diverse and incredible biomes the world has to offer only to be told that you must go through the only socially acceptable form of hazing that still exists: Interning. More specifically, being told to do demeaning, trivial, or disgusting tasks for real scientists while they get their names on papers and do blow with the natives. "Sure, you can come with us to the topless waterfalls to collect tree frogs but first we need you to stab microscopic tire pumps into about a thousand rats for tomorrow's test." "Like into their arms?" "Hah, No..."

Sharon (actual scientist in white coat) shows John (just an intern, lame blue coat LOL) where exactly to stick the needle into the rat erection. John is adding up the many tens of thousands of dollars in tuition he has paid in order to get to this point, and not at all regretting it, as evidenced by his expression.
Photo: US DoE Savannah River Site

Dying Of Old Age Means Ripping Your Own Arms Off

You could be an **octopus.** Yes, you would be the smartest invertebrate in the world; and yes, you could instantly change your color and texture to disappear into your surroundings; and yes, you could use tools, fit through any space larger than your freakish beaked mouth and fart ink clouds, but all that awesomeness comes at a seriously messed up cost.

Octopuses* die after mating in a fairly brutal and spectacular way. For the males, it is pretty straight forward. They basically just starve themselves to death. The females also stop eating but must still care for their eggs before permanently checking out. The mother octopus guards her nursery and cleans the eggs until it is very close to hatching time. As the date approaches, the female's body starts to rapidly degrade, and she will aid this full-body Alzheimer's routine by tearing off her own limbs and chewing herself up. This process seems to be involuntary and controlled by chemical signals triggered through the brooding process.

When the eggs finally do hatch, it is not uncommon for the baby octopus's first sight to be the grey, bloated, dismembered body of one or both of their parents swaying in the current. Scientists believe that the reason for this is that God is a bastard. An alternative theory is that octopuses must be culled by their own brains after mating to prevent them from eating their young, as octopuses are unapologetically cannibalistic by nature.

Left: A giant pacific octopus before having kids. Right: a giant pacific octopus after having kids. Notice the lack of pigment, white lesions and general sort of dying vibe. If that isn't the best argument for birth control, I don't know what is. Photos (left to right): Bill Abbott, Youtube CBC

*Yes, it is octopuses. Octopi is wrong because it is Latin, and the word octopus comes from Greek. Octopodes is technically correct as a Greek suffix, but it also happens to be very stupid-sounding.

You Could Have Parents Who Would Literally Rather Die Than Take Care Of You

You could be a baby octopus that can read and be given this book as a Christmas present and learn that evolution gave your mom two choices. A) don't eat your own goddamn baby and live a long and fruitful life as the smartest thing without a backbone, or B) do eat your own children and slowly degenerate while simultaneously starving to death and tearing your own body to ribbons. Your parents would rather waste away in the most brutal way than give up infanticide. Dear old mom didn't even think about it before she went full "127 Hours" and just started hacking limbs off left and right. Baby octopuses live with the incredibly depressing realization that their parents would rather cannibalize them than live longer than a county fair goldfish. They also have to worry about everybody else in the ocean wanting to eat them too. The average octopus will lay eighty-thousand eggs before plucking itself to pieces. Of those eighty-thousand babies less than ten will survive to adulthood.

Top 5 Worst Things To Find Out About Your Parents

1. **Kim Kardashian's** kids finding out how their entire family's fortune came from a poorly lit home video of mommy and **Ray J** "playing house."

2. Finding your dad's old war uniform buried under your porch in **Argentina** and realizing why all the people in your town speak **German** instead of Spanish.

3. Being a baby octopus and finding out why you are an orphan.

4. **Adam and Eve's** grandkids finding out why their parents look so similar.

5. Praying mantis kids hearing what really happened to their dad from the other bugs at school.

You Could Have Exploding Testicles

You could be a male **honey bee** (*Apis mellifera*) who finds a mate. The sole purpose in the life of **drones** (male honeybees) is to find a mate. To this end, they do not help the completely female workforce of a honeybee colony collect nectar or pollen. In fact, they do not do any domestic work in the hive at all (think human males for most of human history). Additionally, drones do not have stingers, and so cannot fight or defend anything (think most human males now). For these reasons, they are viewed as being fairly expendable (just like your stepdad once the disability checks stop coming). At this point, I could hardly fault you for agreeing that the male honeybee is a bit of a freeloader except he didn't choose the bum life, the bum life chose him.

His body is much different from the female worker bee's. While females have special adaptations to help them gather pollen, store and refine nectar into honey, and secrete wax for honeycomb, the drone's body is built for hunting down that sweet, sweet honeybee ass. He is essentially a massive pair of eyes on top of flying gonads. Each day he leaves the colony with a full belly (honey and sperm) in search of a virgin queen to mate with. If he succeeds, he will join her in a mid-air mating ritual that culminates in his gonads literally exploding. This is apparently an effective way to transfer his seed. This process is always fatal (I hope) to the drone and must be a little awkward for the -no longer- virgin queen. Additional drones drawn in by the queen's pheromones will continue to literally bust their nuts all over her until she has gathered enough sperm to last her the rest of her life. Say what you will about your first time but at least nobody died during the climax. (Again, I hope.)

List of some of the incredible adaptations that female honeybees have in order to help them survive and aid their colony:

1. Tarsal baskets to hold pollen.

2. Pheromone secreting glands to aid in communication.

3. Abdominal glands for creating and secreting wax for honeycomb

4. Stinger for colony defense

5. Ability to navigate great distances and remember food sources.

6. Surprisingly complex brain capable of understanding communication, simple math, reasoning and problem solving.

7. Muscles that can detach from wings on command in order to produce heat without moving air.

8. Specialized mouthparts able to mix nectar and saliva to make honey.

9. Second stomach for storing nectar without consuming it.

List of male honeybee adaptations:

1. Self-destructing balls

Photo: Nate Ramos

Photo: Waugsberg

Photo: Michael L. Smith

Right: see all those gut-looking things coming out of the drone's butt? That is his endo-phallus. Endo-phallus is Greek (probably) for "inside-penis". You will notice this one is not "endo" the drone's body at all, in fact, it is quite "ecto" his body. Consequently, this drone is very dead.

Your Family Could Murder You Because You're A Virgin

Such is the fate of any male honeybee who does not find a mate. While it is true that remaining celibate will prevent death by exploding gonads, it is hard to say that the drones who are unsuccessful in finding a mate are any better off. For starters, they have managed to not get laid when it is not only their sole motivation in life but also their actual nine-to-five job. Their only consolation is that the humiliation will be short-lived. As we've established, drones do not do any work inside the hive. When winter comes and it is time to live off the stored honey that was so carefully prepared by the girls all summer, it seems that female bees are not very tolerant of mooches. The "loser drones" as they are called, are unceremoniously dragged out of the hive by their family and left to freeze to death. Re-entry into the hive is barred, and any males trying to come inside to eat or stay warm are violently harassed and mobbed by their sisters. So, if you are a honeybee drone, no matter what happens during your summer you will die by the end of it, and neither option is going to be pleasant.

Pictured above: A typical honeybee drone's end of summer calendar.

You Could Be A Chicken-Sized Bird Who Lays Ostrich-Sized Eggs

We are talking about the **kiwi bird**. The kiwi is a member of the **ratite** family, which includes the ostrich, the emu and the cassowary. This widespread group of birds comprises remnants from a time immediately following the **dinosaur's** extinction. With no more giant nightmare-inducing lizards to fly away from, the ratites figured why fly at all? Which is how you know they were stupid. (For more on birds that spit in the face of the coolest adaptation that nature ever came up with, see the entry on **penguins**.) Without the necessity to stay trim and light enough for take-off, the ratites were free to bulk up and get larger and heavier. The largest members of this family were truly enormous. The giant moa* could be 12ft tall and the elephant bird could weigh as much as 880lbs. Imagine having that thing for Thanksgiving dinner. You would have to start defrosting the damn thing in August.

The modern-day ratites are not as large, but they are still massive compared to their bird brethren. All of them except for the kiwi, that is. In order of size, the ostrich clocks in at 9 ft tall, and around 310 lbs. in weight. The Australian emu can be 6 ft, 110 lbs. Cassowaries are usually shorter but much heavier, sometimes reaching 180lbs. The rhea of South America can be 4.5 ft tall and weigh as much as 80 lbs. The kiwi is not even close to its cousins, only being about the size of a chicken. The average kiwi stands an average of 1.5ft tall and weighs a scant 4.5lbs.

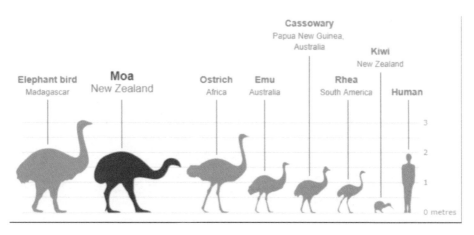

A size comparison chart of current and extinct ratite birds. Notice the size difference between the Ostrich (3rd from left) and the kiwi (dumb little one next to the person) seeing the size difference between those birds and the lack of difference in their eggs is like if a five-year-old kid took the same size shits as Shaq.

Evolution shrunk everything on the kiwi. Not only are they the smallest members of their families, but of any bird species, kiwi eyes are the smallest, in proportion to their body. In fact, kiwi eyes are so under-developed that a third of specimens observed in a study were found to be completely blind. Kiwis are nocturnal and while most animals that hunt at night have developed exceptional eyesight to help with this, the kiwi just said, "Screw it; I'll just sort of poke around with my beak and smell for my food." Which would not have been my route, but whatever. Kiwi birds also got the short end of the femur when it comes to protection. Whereas the ostrich can defend itself with its great speed and bone-shattering kicks and the cassowary can and has killed an adult man with its large talons, the kiwi has neither of these options. Instead, the kiwi's only defense against predators was to not have any. Kiwis stuck to islands in the Pacific where there were no large predators and just sort of crossed their not-fingers and prayed. That strategy worked great until people introduced **cats** to **New Zealand**, and the hungry felines proceeded to merc the defense-less, flightless and often blind kiwis right onto the endangered species list. Fucking cats…

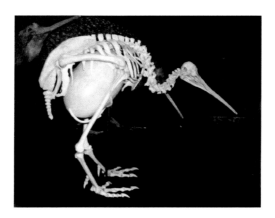

Kiwi skeleton with egg. Notice the lack of room inside the ribcage for things like organs and space for your lungs to fill with air. My question is like, why?

It seems that whenever evolution offered to shrink something on the kiwi, the latter said, "Sure." Working wings? Overrated! Operational eyeballs? Who needs them? Intimidating body size? You can keep it! There was nothing that the kiwi wasn't willing to give up in the pursuit of being the lamest version of a ratite. That is, except for one thing. Its massive, wince-inducing egg size. The kiwi's egg is almost the exact same size as an ostrich's, weighing in at one pound or about 25 percent the weight of the kiwi's entire body. That is the equivalent of a human giving birth to a forty-two pound baby. The kiwi's eye-watering egg-to-body-size ratio is by far the largest of any bird and there doesn't seem to be any good reason for it. The kiwi is small enough to get murdered by a domestic cat but through gross evolutionary oversight must painfully squeeze out an egg large enough to make an omelet for a family of four all while being legally blind; flapping useless, atrophied wings; and being picked on for being the only dwarf in a family of giants.

*Say what you will about how shitty modern humans are, but people have been kill-ing off cool shit long before your great grand-dad discovered **deforestation**. The giant moa didn't go extinct until 1445, when Māori natives arrived on New Zealand and deep-fried them into extinction.*

You Could Have Been The First Dog To Die In Outer Space

Imagine yourself as a particularly unlucky stray **dog** living in **Moscow, Russia** in 1957. After being picked up by a group of **Soviet scientists**, along with all the other strays they could find, you would have been subjected to a series of increasingly confusing tests. First you would have been put through a series of exercises to ensure you were agreeable and docile. Once that was established, you and the rest of the nice ones would have been fed a special diet of nutrient-rich gelatin and fitted with a doggie-diaper. Most of your fellow guinea pig-dogs would eventually fail out because they refused to shit in a bag tied to their waist like a disgusting human. However, some of the dogs would have been like, "Beats eating turnips out the trash during a Moscow winter" and gone with it. Next, the **Soviets** would have put you in a **centrifuge** to see how well the lights stayed on up in your noggin while **G-forces** were applied. Only yourself and one other dog would pass. In between spinning sessions, they would house you in ever smaller and smaller cages until you had no room to move while resting. You would have kept waking up with bald spots and stitches, and unbeknownst to you they would have fitted you with several monitors to study your heart rate and breathing. After all this, the scientists would have put you and your colleague up on a table and voted. They decided that they liked the other dog better and so you would be selected for the mission. At this point, you would have been awfully worried that you won a contest because you were *less* likable than your comrade and would have started barking for answers. That barking would have caught some attention, and people would start calling you "barker," which in Russian translates to **Laika.**

If the name Laika sounds familiar it is because she became the first animal to orbit the Earth successfully. Unfortunately, she was not the first animal to *return* to Earth successfully. Alas, the Soviets had no plans to bring her back alive nor did they have the ability to. Her capsule was designed to run out of air after seven days, at which point, she would slip into unconsciousness and die peacefully. However, spaceflight was still in its spit-in-the-face-of-God's-will, heaven-defying-infancy, so poor Laika never got the chance to asphyxiate. Instead, her heatshield burned up and she cooked alive somewhere between the second and fourth lap of the Earth. I know that this story is kind of really fucked-up for the dog lovers out there, but you should know that Laika did not get air-fried for nothing. Because of her unwitting sacrifice, Russians proved once and for all that dogs cannot survive space travel once they cook to about medium-rare.

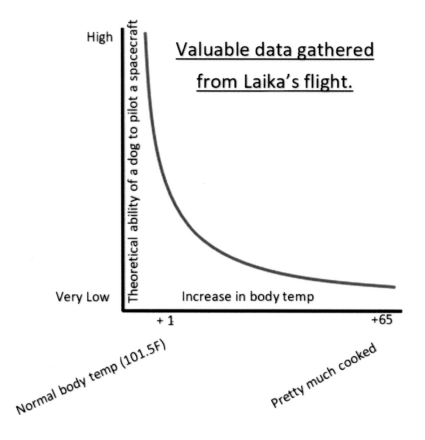

You Could Have Been Any of The Other Involuntary Astronauts Sent To The Great Pet Cemetery In The Sky

When I say dead animals, I really mean one of the dozens and dozens of other "astro-nots" that went to space alive and came back dead in the years following Laika's fateful orbit. These unlucky animals suffered strange and often gruesome deaths all so that the United States and U.S.S.R could compete for the title of "middle finger to the other guy officially flung the furthest from the rock it was born on."

It is possibly worth noting that most of these animals died accidentally, as by this point both sides had moved on from proving whether you could survive leaving Earth and were working out how to survive landing on it again. As it turns out, flinging animals into space is easier than catching animals that were dropped from space.

Actual Conversation in the 1960's: "Mother! Is that a shooting star?"
"No, it's a golden retriever sweetheart."

You Could Be The Dumbest Mammal On Earth And Also In A Perpetual Food Coma

The animal I'm describing is the **koala bear.** I can hear you arguing "What's so bad about getting to sleep all day cuddled up to a tree in sunny **Australia?**" First of all, our species took over the planet after we decided that sleeping in trees sucks ass. Secondly, the koala doesn't *get* to sleep all day; it *has* to because the stuff it eats is highly toxic and requires the koala to be in a near-catatonic state in order to be safely digested. That food would be the leaves of the **eucalyptus tree.** Besides being poisonous, eucalyptus leaves are tough, oily and almost completely devoid of nutrition. This unsavory combo of traits means that the koala puts nearly all the energy it gets from its food right back into digesting it.

If that is not enough of an evolutionary short stick, then consider that koalas hold the unenviable title of smoothest brain of any mammal. I don't mean smooth like cool; I mean smooth like missing the foldy bits that increase surface area and make possible the thing that everyone except koalas calls "thinking".

Koala bear (Phascolarctos cinereus) trying its hardest to stay alive after eating its favorite food, poison salad. Photo: Dronepicr

Basically, the Koala is as dumb as a box of rocks if those rocks ate exclusively toxic food. Koalas also have no solution to the problem of their teeth being worn down by the extremely tough leaves they eat. Koalas do not grow replacement teeth or regrow lost tooth enamel, so when their teeth wear down, they starve to death. Lastly, almost all koala bears left in the wild have **chlamydia,** so yeah.

In conclusion, if you think your diet sucks, at least your food isn't so toxic that you are forced to go catatonic in order to eat it. Taco Bell technically counts, but you don't *have* to eat that; you *choose* to. You shouldn't though. We should all boycott Taco Bell until they bring back the quesorito. You hear me Taco Bell?! I know you have the stuff for it, you bastards! Your whole menu has the same 5 ingredients.

You Could Be A
Vegan Carnivore

Speaking of bears that aren't bears you could be a panda bear. Unlike koalas who are definitely not bears, the **giant panda** is actually a proper bear of the same family as grizzlies and polar bears. But is it, though? I ask because it is seriously bad at being one. The panda, along with all true bears, is a member of the order Carnivora, but unlike pretty much everyone else in that group, it does not eat meat.

To be clear, pandas could eat meat if they wanted to because they are fucking bears with bear teeth and bear claws and bear guts, but they don't. Instead, they subsist almost exclusively on bamboo shoots and leaves. Their bear guts are not very good at digesting bamboo though, and so they get only about 17 percent of the available calories present in their food. This means that they must eat a lot and pass it quickly to make room for more. Pandas eat up to 230 lbs. of bamboo shoots a day and take up to forty bamboo shits in the same time period. Imagine a turd made 100 percent from poorly digested wood fiber being pushed out of your ass forty times a day!

And then there's the sex (or lack thereof). Possibly because they are too busy eating and shitting, female pandas are only fertile for three days in a year. Knowing this, you would think that males and females would hang out in groups or pairs or at least within earshot of one another but they don't. Pandas are solitary and often by the time a male finds the trail of a female in heat, the window for conception has closed. If he does actually find her in time, he must overcome the smallest penis-to-body ratio of any of the bear species. I will admit that this is a shitty thing to call them out for but, it is true. If everything goes right, the panda will raise a single cub and teach it to eat the same stupid diet that the momma does, and so the cycle continues. Notice that I said *"raise one cub"* and not *"give birth to* one cub". Multiple births happen fairly regularly, but momma pandas will abandon all but one of the newborns on each occasion. I find this to be an interesting strategy for an animal battling extinction but that's stupid frickin pandas for you.

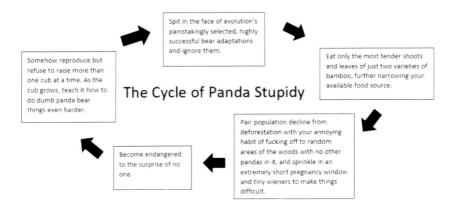

Spit in the face of evolution's painstakingly selected, highly successful bear adaptations and ignore them.

Eat only the most tender shoots and leaves of just two varieties of bamboo, further narrowing your available food source.

Somehow reproduce but refuse to raise more than one cub at a time. As the cub grows, teach it how to do dumb panda bear things even harder.

The Cycle of Panda Stupidy

Pair population decline from deforestation with your annoying habit of fucking off to random areas of the woods with no other pandas in it, and sprinkle in an extremely short pregnancy window and tiny wieners to make things difficult.

Become endangered to the surprise of no one.

You Could Have The World's Most Self-Sabotaging Mascot

Imagine being some poor **philanthropist schmuck** donating big money to The **World Wildlife Fund** and then finding out that the face of the foundation is something so bad at existing that it is eating itself into extinction by choice. I mean, of all the animals who were severely screwed over by humans, they picked an animal ambassador getting killed by its own fad diet. "Please give us money so that we can save an animal that has been slowly and intentionally getting worse at surviving for tens of thousands of years. If we do nothing the panda bear will go extinct. If we do a lot it will probably still go extinct but like... naturally."

*Much like asking **Osama Bin Laden** to cut commercials for the **TSA** or
Kanye West teaming up with the **Anti-Defamation League,** pairing the idiotic
panda bear with the World Wildlife Fund is a terrible collaboration.*

You Could Be In A Race To The Death The Moment You Are Born

You could be a baby **Tasmanian devil** (*Sarcophilus harrisii*). These unenvious little **marsupials** have a rough life, and it starts getting rough pretty much right out of the gate. And when I say "gate," I am referring, of course, to their mother's vagina.

You see, marsupials like kangaroos, dumbass koalas and Tasmanian devils cannot produce a **placenta.** This is problematic for developing embryos because one of the functions of a placenta (besides being the most disgusting and least forgettable part of witnessing your child's birth) is that it protects a fetus from the mother's immune system. Because of their mother's lack of evolutionary oversight, baby marsupials must leave their mother's womb after just a few weeks and finish developing somewhere safe from **Osmosis Jones** and his buddies*.

Imagine being a developing devil baby (of the Tasmanian variety, not Rosemary's**) and having to leave the womb because your mom is trying to digest you. Because you've only been growing for a few days, you must do this before you have eyes, ears, fur, or pretty much anything other than front legs. You are basically a reverse tadpole. You wriggle your way out of the vagina and make your way down to momma devil's pouch where you will latch on to one of four nipples approximately the size of your entire body. Once you do, the nipple will swell inside your mouth, permanently attaching itself to you for the rest of your development. You must make this journey from womb to pouch quickly for two reasons: Firstly, you need to finish growing a lot of organs and eyeballs and other junk and that is hard to do outside, in the elements. Secondly, you have lots of competition. Tasmanian devils have a ludicrously large litter size of between twenty and thirty babies in each pregnancy and only two pairs of nipples to feed them with. So, you and up to twenty-nine of your little nightcrawlers-with-hands siblings are in a race to the death where it is critically important to finish fourth or better.

This picture is not advertising a four for the price of one deal on abortions at Planned Parenthood. Rather, it is actually showing how small and useless a newborn Tasmanian devil is when it is forced to race all 30 of its siblings for a spot at the dinner table.

For the non-millennials in the audience, Osmosis Jones was the titular character in a 2001 animated buddy-cop documentary that very accurately depicts how white blood cells like Osmosis Jones act as the police force of Bill Murray's body, cleaning up the streets/veins and protecting him from viruses.

** For the non-baby boomers in the audience, Rosemary was the titular character in a 1968 rom-com film called "**Rosemary's Baby**" in which a pregnant woman loses her mind before giving birth to the actual devil's baby who is then kidnapped by cultists. It is a real laugh riot.

You Could Win A Race To The Death The Moment You Are Born And Eat Poop-Shoots For A Living As The Prize

If you are a Tasmanian devil that finishes between first and fourth places and gets to live long enough to watch your legs finish growing, don't start jumping for joy just yet. If you do survive the worst P.E. test ever, life is not exactly easy for a young devil.

For one thing, adult Tasmanian devils are cannibalistic and will happily try to finish the job that your mother's severe lack of **mammary glands** started. If you do not get eaten by one of your relatives the moment you tumble backwards out of mother's pouch, then you will happily take up the Tasmanian devil's chosen profession of eating everything and anything that it can fit into its gaping, bone-crushing jaws. Tasmanian devils do hunt but they get most of their calories from scavenging off carrion, garbage and **roadkill**. Eating garbage is not my cup of tea, but someone must keep the bodies from piling up and considering how the Tasmanian devil primarily ate before people came along, it is no wonder why they will happily chew on empty take-out containers, old shoes and rotten leftovers.

Although it is nearly impossible to see, there is a Tasmanian devil in this picture, perfectly camouflaged against the asphalt behind him.
Photo: Tasmanian Environment Department

Without human trash to eat, Tasmanian devils like to share a carcass with friends. That's a nice sentiment, but like I tell children who stray too close to me at Chuck E. Cheese, sharing is a **zero-sum game.** Nobody knows that better than Tasmanian devils. If you are a devil with dinner guests you need to fill up quick before the bloated, maggot-ridden wombat carcass gets gobbled up without you. Doing this means getting to the good stuff quickly. If you are a disgusting Tasmanian devil, this means going ass-to-mouth in a very literal culinary sense. Tasmanian devils will almost always start by disemboweling their prey, chomping down on the turd-cutter, and working their way further into the body cavity until they are completely inside of the prey item. Once inside, they will continue to eat from the inside out until they are completely gorged or until they run out of entrails to consume. Only after the guts are gone will the Tasmanian devil start going after the boring cuts like rumps and ribeye. The practice of starting your digestive process where someone else's ends is actually not that uncommon amongst scavengers, but it must really be engrained in Tasmanian devil culture because literally every source I used felt the need to mention how common it is to see a Tasmanian devil with its back feet sticking out of the butthole of some unfortunate piece of roadkill.

Speaking of roadkill, the Tasmanian devil is the victim of vehicle strikes as much as it is the benefactor of them. There are a couple of reasons for this. For one, it is very hard to hear a car coming while you are chewing. It is even more difficult to do so when you are listening for that car from inside the anal cavity of your meal. Secondly, and more tragically, Tasmanian devils happen to be very hard to see at night because they are completely black with a white stripe across their backside. One could describe this arrangement as being dangerously "road colored." Between being pavement patterned and taking your meals in the middle of the thoroughfare, the chances of being un-alived by a car are tragically high for a Tasmanian devil.

If you aren't turned into a skid mark by a Toyota, eaten by your in-laws as a child, or starved to death by your siblings during a game of musical chairs/nipples minutes after being born, your most likely cause of death will come from beef with a human. Well, technically the problem is mutton not beef. **European colonizers** believed that Tasmanian devils were killing their sheep, and until very recently humans systematically hunted and poisoned the Tasmanian devils to near extinction. Now, while you do not get named after Satan without causing your fair share of problems, it is now believed that most examples of Tasmanian devils feeding on sheep were examples of scavenging, not predation. It is a bit ironic that a creature that is willing to go after just about anything was almost hunted to extinction because of the one thing it didn't prey on.

If all that wasn't enough, there are two last little F-U goodie bags that the Tasmanian devil received from evolution. We have already talked about their disgusting little feeding habit of starting every dinner with the worst kind of rim-job imaginable, but we didn't fully discuss the implications of this. Tasmanian devils have an exceptional sense of smell. Their extremely sensitive nose is located right where you would expect it to be: on the end of their face. That puts their nose right at the front door when the anal buffet line opens. I don't think I can stress enough that an animal that has an extremely sensitive nose eats carrion, ass-first. That is as if you were born with the world's most sensitive gums and your favorite food was broken glass.

To add insult to injury, apparently Tasmanian devils are one of the world's smelliest animals. I know what you are thinking "Yeah, no shit, they are basically butt plugs with teeth how could they possibly smell good?" But this smell is not *on* them; it comes *from* them. When threatened, a Tasmanian devil will exude an extremely potent, foul-smelling odor from glands on its body. So not only do they suffer through each poop-scented meal with their incredibly acute sense of smell, but they also use an offensive odor as a defense mechanism. That is like getting mugged and kicking the bad guy in the balls and then spraying yourself with pepper spray. It might work, but at what cost?

Last but certainly not least, the few Tasmanian devils that do not die at the hands of a relative, or from shaking hands with a moving Land Cruiser have an extremely good chance of dying from a disfiguring form of cancer that causes painful, weeping tumors on their faces. This particular cancer is doubly insidious because it is transmissible. Devils can acquire the disease from contacting an infected specimen and so the most aggressive devils are the most likely to become mutilated. Part of me thinks god genuinely got confused and thought that Tasmanian devils are the actual devil and so he has just been hurling metaphorical thunderbolts at them since the ice age. The other part of me thinks that you can only stick your face in so many orifices it does not belong in before you catch some kind of something.

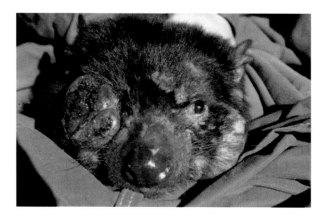

The disgusting protrusion on this Tasmanian devil's head is actually not a bloody marshmallow that someone left over the fire for too long. Instead, it is a perfect-if-graphic example of Devil Facial Tumor Disease. Photo: Menna Jones

In conclusion, Tasmanian devils are car-magnet, cannibalistic, cancer-ridden, self-sabotaging, creatures with a terrible diet and an even worse public relations team who should probably go extinct for their own good and you are lucky to not be one.

You Could Be A Public Toilet But Also Alive

You could be the tree that groups of Tasmanian devils use as a "community latrine." Here you are, just minding your own business and making life-sustaining oxygen for everybody, and a roaming gang of devils starts shitting all over you. Apparently, troupes of devils use a specific tree in the center of their over-lapping territories as an above-ground toilet. They take turns defecating around it and also climbing the branches and pooping in the tree itself to really help the aroma waft better. Scientists disagree as to the motivation behind deciding as a group to decorate the world's shittiest Christmas tree (pun intended) but those scientists almost universally believe that this shared behavior is a dick move.

Imagine that the baubles are poop and the little white tree ornaments are poop and the snowmen are poop. That is what passes for a Christmas tree in the Tasmanian devil community. Photo: freestocks.org

You Could Be A Fucking Tree

I can't even really wrap my head around how much it would suck to be a tree. Imagine if you were on a hike with your girlfriend, and you saw a pig, and you thought you would remember the moment by carving your initials into the side of the pig. You wouldn't be able to because the pig would run away, but trees aren't pigs. They just have to sit there and take it. Similarly, if a bird tried to build a nest on your shoulder you would swat it away and move. Trees just have to listen to a gaggle of baby birds tweeting incessantly and endure getting shit on by them.

Picture this sequence of events happening to you as if you were a tree. First, a bug tunnels under your skin and starts chewing on the underlying flesh. Then a woodpecker comes and starts stabbing the shit out of you until it makes a big enough wound to reach the aforementioned bug and eats it. Then the bird continues stabbing you until the hole is big enough to sit inside of and it proceeds to raise a family there. When the woodpecker leaves, a squirrel comes along and stuffs a bunch of acorns and random bullshit inside the gaping wound. Down by your ankles, a man takes a drill and bores a hole into your leg just deep enough to get a steady stream of blood. He hooks up a bucket and collects enough blood to fill the bucket without killing you. He then takes that blood and boils it down and spreads it on pancakes. Dogs come by and piss on you to mark their territory. A deer walks up and scratches off all your skin to mark his territory. Later, a guy comes along and nails a sign to your ass to mark *his* territory. Back up top, the squirrel has come back for his nuts, and the now rotten wound is softened up enough to let other animals hollow it out even more. An owl spends a season there. A family of raccoons carves out a little more, and takes up residence, and the entire time you can't do a goddamn thing about it.

Just the number of ironic scenarios involving the unfortunate side effect of being both really useful for making things out of and also being alive is enough. For instance, I'm certain that someone somewhere has written a book warning about the terrors of deforestation on paper that was made from the pulverized body of a tree that has (had) been alive for longer than the printing press has been around. That would be like someone writing a book about how important panda bears are (you shouldn't because they aren't.) and you printed the book on the stretched and dried skins of juvenile panda. Actually... I would probably buy that... little black and white fur for a dust cover, binding made from bamboo fibers...

Anyway, I'm getting off track. This section is supposed to be about how animals are terrible to trees, and by "animals" I mean proper animals not humans- and when I say proper animals- I am also excluding phone scammers, child molesters, and the lazy cretons who don't push their carts back even though all of these exceptions are technically examples of non-human beasts. The multitude of ways in which animals are terrible to trees is so varied and numerous that it boggles the mind. Thank heavens we are the lumberjacks and not the lumber-jacked.

You Could Die A Virgin
Because You're A Virgin

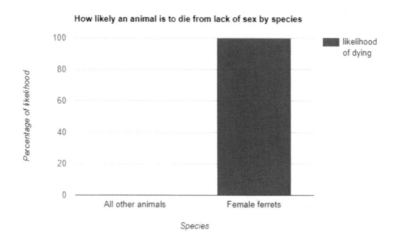

How likely an animal is to die from lack of sex by species

A graph showing how screwed ferrets are by not getting screwed.

Such is the plight of the lady **ferret.** Ferrets are basically furry slinkies with nipples, which has nothing to do with fatal celibacy, but it is my favorite way of visualizing them. The trouble with being a female ferret in particular is one of sex or more accurately, not having sex. You see, when a human does not have sex for a long time they just spend all day on 4Chan or become a priest. When a female ferret does not have sex for a long time, she fucking dies. That's right. When a ferret goes into heat, her body ramps up the free **estrogen** in her body. This helps kick off a number of physiological changes necessary for pregnancy, but it has a bad side effect. The excess estrogen causes her bones to stop producing marrow and red blood cells.

Ferrets are somewhat unique among mammals in that once they start **estrus** (technical term for being "in heat"), they will stay in estrus until they are impregnated. This isn't a problem if a suitable mate is around because once they do the nasty, everything is good. Her estrogen levels will fall, and her body will stop trying to kill her from the skeleton on out. However, if the lady ferret finds herself without a partner, she will develop **aplastic anemia** and die from blue balls.

Can you imagine how many things would disappear if you could die from not having sex? No more adult spelling bees, no IRS, no identity thieves, no **Runescape,** no **TMZ,** no professional content moderators, no real life quidditch clubs, no **PT Cruisers** and no more calls about my car's extended warranty. All these rich cultural achievements are only possible because human virgins are allowed to reach adulthood.

Apart from the obvious buzz kill of dying from not getting laid, female ferrets have the very disturbing adaptation that does not let them ovulate until they have been abused by their sexual partner. Yeah, WTF, right? A male ferret will pin a female to the ground and bite her head and drag her around until she submits to him and this is actually necessary to get certain hormones flowing for the baby making.

I'm not sure which world view disturbs me more when processing this fact. On one hand, you could believe that evolution eventually found the perfect amount of spousal violence needed to create a reproductive advantage, which implies that a lot of ferret couples were just aggressively toxic and it was accidentally beneficial. Alternatively, you could believe that a loving and benevolent higher power gave one of their creations the choice between being beaten and bloodied instead of experiencing foreplay or running out of red blood cells and dying a virgin. Either way, that is messed up.

Ferret porn is very specific and pretty dark. It is pretty much just the one category.
Ferret Logo by Jan Prill

You Could Only Knock Up Your Old Lady By Knocking Her Down

Imagine being a male ferret just trying to start a family with the missus, and she tells you that it won't work if you don't rough her up before-hand. So out of love, you start throwing haymakers at your spouse like an NFL player on CCTV, and everybody on the prairie starts going, "Woah man, not cool man, not cool at all man!" They start filming you instead of calling the police or stepping in but you are glad they don't step in because you are just trying to do it the way ferrets do it, but now the video is viral; and you lose your job; and your family won't speak to you; and you were inter-rupted, so you never finished; and so your girlfriend stops making blood and dies.

Those are the stakes if you are a bachelor ferret. The next time you are down on your dating prospects, just be glad you don't have to beat the girl up in order to save her life.

You Could Have Traded The Power Of Flight For Flippers And Then Discovered That Killer Whales Exist

You could be a **penguin.** Ask anyone you know what superpower they would want if they could choose. If they don't choose the ability to fly, they are a psychopath, and I will not be argued with over this.

What if I told you that your ancestors could fly and chose not to so often that they lost the ability to do so? You would ask me which super-power they gained in this tradeoff, and you would be horrified to learn that instead of soaring in the clouds with the trumpeting angels, they can now swim real good in the absolute terror-ridden shit show that is the ocean.

Flippers instead of wings. That is the worst trade ever, and here is why: The ocean is terrifying, and honestly this whole book could just be a list of everything that lives there. I'm not talking about the beaches you see in Sands Resort commercials. I'm talking about the true briny deep. The place where nightmares evolve legs and wriggle onto dry land so that they can invade your dreams. That is where penguins' great-great-great-a-million-times-great grandfathers decided to hang out instead of the air; the place we flush all our shit into, and also there's giant squids down there. You know how many sharks there are in the air? **Orcas?** Leopard seals? Oh no, those are all things that hunt penguins in the water, where they decided to live instead.

Well, at least they don't have to contend with other birds now that they don't fly, except oh wait, one the biggest predators of penguin chicks are giant petrels, which are big ass murderous birds. The real kind of bird that is, the kind that can still fly. Petrels use their- get this- *wings* to fly down and scoop up defenseless, flightless penguin chicks and then use those same working, flying wings to soar away while the penguin parents awkwardly stand around flapping their useless non-flying wings and cursing their ancestors.

Things That Ate Penguins When They Could Fly:	Things That Eat Penguins Now:
• Other birds sometimes.	• Sharks • Killer Whales • Dolphins • Leopard Seals • Big Ass Fish • Sea Lions • Weddell Seals • Snakes • Foxes • Cats • Other birds Sometimes

Objectively a shit trade when you look at the number of predators you inherit as a result.

Your Nursery Could Be -112 Fucking Degrees

You could be an **emperor penguin.** Being a penguin is bad enough, but being the only penguin crazy enough to try to start a family during the brutal Antarctic winter is worth an entry all by itself.

Emperor penguins breed during the winter months because they are psychopaths that enjoy pain and hardship. Emperor penguins are the guy you know that wears shorts in the winter regardless of conditions and claims not to be bothered by the cold, except penguins do it to the extreme.

Emperor penguins leave the ocean, march to their breeding grounds and join colonies of thousands of other horny penguins. Emperor penguins pair up at the start of winter and stay together for the rest of the year while they raise a single chick- hopefully.

By the time the female penguin gestates and then lays her egg, her food reserves are depleted, so she leaves the fresh egg with the male emperor and returns to the sea to feed. The male now huddles over the egg and keeps it warm for the next sixty-five to seventy-five days. This means that daddy penguins must leave the ocean, find a mate, impregnate her, wait for her to lay an egg and then keep that egg alive for a total time of 125 days without sitting or eating once.

Now I am not a bird expert, but I am a pretty good at recognizing bullshit and I get the feeling that the male penguins are getting screwed here. Imagine getting whipped by sustained winds of 90mph in minus forty degrees for two months while your wife is on an ocean cruise, stuffing her face with fresh sushi and shrimp scampi, and you can't even lie down or your baby will freeze to death. You turn to your buddy and go, "Hey, Steve!"

"What's that, Joe? Couldn't hear ya over the category two hurricane winds and -112 **windchill**."

"Yeah, my bad. [shouting now] Hey, Steve!"

"Yeeah?"[also shouting]

"When we all waddled up here together with the girls a while back…"

"Yeeeah?!"

"When we all waddled up here with the girls a while back… how long did it take us to get here?"

[blisteringly cold wind tearing tiny chunks of his face off as he answers] "Oh like a day, maybe two! Why?!"

"Well, the girls have been gone for like almost two months and they said that they were just gonna grab some squid and krill and then come right back to take turns."

"Uh huh… and!?

"Well, doesn't that seem like a long time to be gone when it doesn't take that long to waddle there and back to the ocean, and it doesn't take that long catch a stupid fish for dinner?"

And then Mitch jumps in and says, "Stop talking about food! I'm fucking starving and I can't feel my feet!!!"

And you all look around and realize that your wives are probably sitting on the beach, picking their teeth with a crab claw and laughing their asses off. I can't prove that this is happening, but you've never been to Antarctica, so you don't know either.

The female penguins can't take too long building their fat reserves though, because if the penguin chick hatches before she returns, it will surely die within days. Amazingly, the male emperor penguin has found a work-around to his mate's tardiness as he can produce a chunky, fat-rich solution called crop milk with which he can sustain his child if the mother does not show up before hatching. This solution is temporary though, as he will not be able to create crop milk for more than a week or so due to the fact that he is also starving to death and doesn't have many calories to loan out. Personally, I find it amazing that evolution could give males the ability to make barf-milk in their necks but couldn't be bothered to come up with a child-rearing solution that doesn't involve starving yourself in a frozen hellscape for half of the year.

So, there they are, hundreds or thousands of male penguins, perching an egg on their feet and covering it with a special featherless pouch that sits where you would think the dad's balls should be, sort of smooshing the pouch over the egg and onto his feet. The males huddle together in a tight circle, leaning inward and slowly rotating the outer edge away from the wind in a formation known as the "**turtle formation**" because apparently the term "penguin formation" was taken.

As the circle rotates the outermost- Actually no. I'm sorry, I have to say something- Imagine doing something that nobody else does and working together as a species to overcome the monumental forces of nature, conquering your environment through force of will and adaptation, and scientists name the thing you do after another completely unrelated animal that does not do anything like what you are doing. Turtle formation?! How about "so-fucking-cold-I-have-to be careful when-I-take-a-piss-lest-my-falling-urine-flash-freezes-me-to-the-ground-and-the-whole-formation-slowly-tramples-me-to-death-circle-of-hopelessness-please-god-let-me-die -formation?" Little bit more accurate. Woah, deep breaths… it's not your fault scientists suck at naming things.

*To an **Ornithologist**, this group of miserable birds huddled together for warmth looks exactly like a turtle apparently. Photo: Tessier Ewan*

Anyway, when the "turtle formation" turns, the outermost members slowly shuffle inward, and the inner penguins are slowly forced to the edges. In this way, no individual is exposed to the full brunt of the weather for too long. If during all this shuffling the egg drops and breaks, the male will leave and not return to the colony until the next year. If his mate does not return from her feeding binge with the other females, he will also leave, abandoning the egg to avoid starvation. If the female does come back, the male emperor will transfer the egg or newly hatched chick to the mother and immediately leave to feed himself. In this way, the penguins will alternate shifts of caring for the chick and returning to the sea for food until the chick is old enough to take to the water himself.

I really didn't need to write any of that stuff to convince anyone that it would suck to be an emperor penguin. Why? Because the windchill can be -112 degrees **Fahrenheit** that's why. That is too damn cold to live in and evolution is a cruel whore for making them do it.

You Could Be Born During A Blizzard Oh, No Actually That Is Just The Weather Here

If you have ever lived where **winter** actually means something, and it gets cold and shitty out, then you are familiar with the following scenario. You wake up and you hear the wind howling outside. The forecast says it's only ten degrees out with a -5 windchill. So, you get all bundled up and open the door, and you feel that first blast of frigid air on your face. Your eyes water, your skin bristles, and the edges of your cheeks burn from the cold. You mutter obscenities and tuck your chin into your coat and go to work. That first step into a winter morning sucks ass.

Now imagine that you experience that frozen first step as your literal first step ever. Emperor penguin chicks emerge from their eggs, feel the sub-zero Antarctic winds lashing their newborn faces, and cry out the bird equivalent of "What the fuck is this shit?" before being scooped back into their father's pouch. He will then comfort the whimpering chick by saying, "Don't worry, champ, Mom will be back soon with some food. No, it's not milk, it's way better. It's days-old fish that she is going to puke into your mouth. Won't that be nice?" The chick then spends the next few months gagging on its disgusting food, shivering, and questioning why anything would live in a place where the air hurts this much.

*A **South Pole Skua** eating an emperor penguin chick. This chick is actually one of the lucky ones as it is no longer freezing it's little nutsicles off in a frozen hellscape and subsisting entirely on fish barf. Photo: Denis Luytun*

Before the little frostbitten fluff ball can have its infantile existential crisis, it actually has to make it out of the egg. Many first-time emperor penguins botch the initial transfer of egg from mother to father, and the dropped egg either freezes before they can scoop it up again or cracks on the hardened ground. Imagine dying before you are born because your dad has butterfingers. (Well, buttertoes, I guess.)

If the parents manage not to scramble their child on day one, the developing egg's chances of hatching go up dramatically. However, if the mother gets gobbled up by a leopard seal before returning, it won't matter much.

If his partner does not return once the chick hatches, the father will set it down, and tell it, "Daddy has to go to the store and get some sardines and cigarettes. I'll be right back." The chick then freezes to death while wondering what a cigarette is, and the father emperor penguin goes back to the sea.

Besides the anxiety of always wondering if Mom is running late or if you are about to be an extremely late-term abortion, emperor penguin chicks must look out for kidnappers. It is not uncommon for emperor penguin parents who have lost their own chick to lash out in anguish and steal a chick from another couple. If the kidnappers are successful, the birth parents will split up and return to the sea. In almost all cases though, the kidnappers will eventually lose interest and abandon the chick that they stole which is pretty shitty for everyone but especially for the now completely screwed penguin chick.

If you manage to dodge all of those terrible possibilities and live, then the cycle of suffering begins again. No matter how hard your upbringing was, I am confident that it pales in comparison to the sun-bleached, sub-zero hell hole that emperor penguins are born into.

You Could Have Lost A Race To The South Pole And Then Died There

As bad as it is to be an emperor penguin in Antarctica, it is definitely worse not to be an emperor penguin while in Antarctica. Whereas penguins are very well suited to surviving in the absurd conditions at the bottom of the world, we humans are not. You would think that besides the fact that there is a rather stormy and unpleasant ocean in between us, the barren ice sheets, hurricane-force winds, subzero temperatures and lack of drive-thru liquor stores would be enough to keep humans away from Antarctica. Despite all that, people have never been able to shy away from the chance to plant their flag somewhere and name it after themselves.

At the end of the nineteenth century, the world was running short of places that hadn't had flags planted in them yet, and so lots of eyes were on Antarctica. Specifically, the middle of Antarctica because reaching the South Pole is the explorer equivalent of saying, "Yes, huh times infinity" after someone says, "Nuh -uh times a thousand" in an argument. You can't really one-up someone who has literally been as far away from civilization as you can get without walking back toward it again.

And so it was that British Royal Navy officer and explorer, Robert Falcon Scott made it his mission to attain the southernmost point of the globe on an ill-fated trip to Antarctica in what would become known as the *Terra Nova* Expedition. This exploratory mission to the South Pole aimed to increase our understanding of the continent through a variety of scientific studies and also to bring glory to the British empire by having one of her own be the first person to walk to the middle of the ass-end of the Earth.

Captain Robert Falcon Scott and the four other men of the Terra Nova's polar party photographed at the South Pole. Just look at the joy and sheer giddiness on their sun-burned, frostbitten faces upon learning that they were beaten to the destination. Their evident happiness would not last.
All five men pictured would die on the return from the Pole.

The first part of the mission was a resounding success with the team collecting 2100 animal, plant, and fossil specimens; meteorological information from ice cores; and data supporting the concepts of continental drift and climate change. The second part of the mission was a resounding success as well, except for the part where the *Terra Nova* crew was beaten to the South Pole by a Norwegian team led by a Captain **Roald Amundsen** by thirty-four days. There was also the small caveat of the entire polar party led by Captain Scott dying on the way back to camp.

Imagine hauling your ass across a frozen wasteland for 742 miles, suffering from scurvy, frostbite and a condition endemic to Antarctica known as ThehellamIdoinghere-itis, only to reach your final goal- the most remote location on the planet where no man has ever been- and finding out that somebody has already been. Not only did the Norwegians beat the British expedition to the pole, but they had the audacity to leave a letter addressed to the king of **Norway** that they asked Scott's team to deliver for them. It is not officially known whether this was a tongue-in-cheek form of mockery, but come on, of course it was. Winning a race and then leaving a letter bragging about it at the finish line with a note telling the loser to mail it for you is some next level pre-Internet trolling.

After being beaten to the South Pole, the *Terra Nova* polar party began the grueling march back to their base camp with dwindling supplies, inadequate fuel for their stoves and scurvy in their bones. They carried with them the weight of their failure to reach the Pole first and that damned letter to The King of Norway.

Things started to go wrong at this point- actually pretty much everything had gone wrong for the entire expedition If we're being honest- but the **shitsicle** really started to hit the ice-covered fan right about here. As it turns out, the human body can only suffer through so many hundreds of slogging, frostbitten, malnourished miles before it stops working, and Scott's team found that limit the hard way. When I say "the hard way," I mean "the frozen solid way" because that's how their corpses were found, buried under the snow in a collapsed tent the following spring.

I wonder what Captain Scott and his doomed colleagues would have thought of the fact that not only did the Nordic team reach the pole first (and survive), but they were so well-provisioned and equipped that their team actually gained weight on their return journey. Volumes have been written comparing the British and Nordic teams, but it can be grossly oversimplified by this non-historian as basically coming down to two important factors. Strategy and skill.

Scott's *Terra Nova* expedition relied on a complicated three-tier transport and hauling system that involved nineteen ponies with snow shoes; two dog teams; and three very heavy, unreliable motor sledges (think 1909's equivalent of the world's shittiest snow mobile), as well as stationing provisions along the eventual route at supply depots. Multiple teams of scientists also did lots of collecting and surveying and **kidnapping** of penguin eggs. (Not kidding, some of Scott's men stole three emperor penguin eggs in the winter of 1910 and had to spend months surviving in an igloo before returning to their base camp.)

A man-hauling party pulling a sledge of supplies across deep snow during the Terra Nova Expedition. This picture is a perfect visual representation of the phrase, "Fuck that."

Anyways, Scott's confusing-ass plan unsurprisingly went tits up mostly because all the ponies kept dying, the dog-sled driver didn't know how to drive dogs, and the motor sledges kept failing. One of the sledges actually fell through the sea ice and was lost, and the other two kept breaking down. This was extra problematic because they'd left the sledge mechanic in New Zealand. This meant that Scott's *Terra Nova* team ended up man-hauling pretty much all their food and heavy-ass fossil samples on their backs for thousands of miles.

In contrast, the Norwegian expedition opted for a very straight-for-ward approach. They brought lots of skis and lots of dog sleds and just did what Norwegian people do in the wintertime in slightly colder conditions. The Norwegians also opted to not spend any time picking up rocks or abducting emperor penguin chicks from their confused fathers and just went straight for the South Pole.

As far as skill goes, the British team members refused to learn to ski, decided against using the pony-snowshoes that had been specifically designed for this voyage, and never bothered to learn how to drive a dog sled or repair their motor sledges. Now these are all things I personally would have figured out how to do *before* freezing my balls off in the snowy taint of the world but what do I know? I'm just a writer who isn't frozen solid in the fetal position under a few feet of ice and penguin shit. The Norwegians for their part, also thought that was silly, and just brought only people who already knew how to ski and drive dog sleds.

You Could Have Been A Horse Brought To The South Pole By Some Humans And Then Die There

At least if you are a human and someone asks you if you want to go on an eight-hundred mile hike in Antarctica, you can tell them to go pound sand. Beasts of burden typically do not have much say where and when they are burdened. Remember those nineteen **Siberian ponies** that were taken on the *Terra Nova* polar expedition as pack animals? Well, as I said, these particularly unfortunate pack animals would all die during the expedition through a variety of calamities, not the least of which being that they were chosen to go to Antarctica to pull peoples shit around in minus 40-degree weather for two goddamn years.

Now I realize many people have emotional attachments to horses, so I will attempt to be respectful and delicate in my vivid descriptions of their demise as well as to refer to each pony by the adorable names given to them by the explorers. So, here we go:

Michael the pony (right... duh) with his handler Apsley Cherry-Gerard posing during a rare break in between horrible things happening on the Terra Nova expedition, 1911.

Ponies Davy and Jones were both euthanized after breaking their legs during a storm at sea before reaching Antarctica. (They were in the ship during the storm, just to be clear; they did not break their legs while swimming to the South Pole.)

Blucher was shot after collapsing from exhaustion during the initial supply-laying trip and eaten. Blossom fell to her death at the bottom of a crevasse.

Guts drowned after being tied up on an ice floe that broke loose.

Punch and Uncle Bill both fell into the water in the same incident and were killed via icepick blows from their handlers so that they would not be eaten alive by the orcas who had gathered around them. You read that correctly; human history includes a first-hand account of killer whales eating a fucking horse in Antarctica.

Nobby survived this absurd and terrifying ordeal but never lost the horrified look in his eyes. (Well, not at least until he was shot by the crew and eaten later that same winter.)

Weary Willie became very weary and fell repeatedly before dying in the night.

Hackenschmidt's cause of death is officially unknown, but the leading theory is that he died because he was a pony in Antarctica.

Jehu, Chinaman, Christopher, Victor and Michael succumbed to exhaustion, were shot within days of each other, and then eaten.

The remaining five ponies- Nobby, James Pigg, Snatcher, Snippets and Bones -were also shot to save them from starving once their feed ran out. They were also eaten.

At one point, while there were still some horses left, a crewmember suggested that Captain Scott should shoot the weaker ponies so they could be used to feed the dogs and thereby also conserve dwindling hay for the stronger horses. Captain Scott disagreed vehemently, citing an aversion to "animal cruelty." Thank God he didn't do anything cruel to those ponies, otherwise they wouldn't be able to starve to death while carrying his shit in an ice-hurricane.

You Could Have Been Some Dogs Brought By Humans To The South Pole And Then Die There

You could have been one of Amundsen's dogs. You see, while Captain Scott of the British expedition refused to shoot his ponies before thoroughly starving and overworking them, Captain Roald Amundsen of the Norwegian polar expedition did not have such hang-ups. Amundsen fully acknowledged that he had no plans to return with all his dogs. Instead, he would run the dogs until they were exhausted and then shoot them and feed them to the next dog team. If that sounds incredibly barbaric and also extremely efficient that's because it is!

Two of Captain Amundsen's favorite dogs "Fix" and "Lassesin" pictured in Antarctica during his South Pole expedition in 1911. We know they are his favorites presumably because they are not pictured as cubes of meat in a stew.

"Excuse me, Captain! [imagine they are speaking whatever oofy-doof language they speak in Norway] I could not help but notice that we have neglected to bring any kibble for our dogs. We must stop and take on provisions."

"Sven, I told you, the dogs *are* the dog food… obviously."

"Oh yes, I thought you were kidding about that, and also that you were insane. Never mind, I'll just feed these dogs to each other and not be horrified about it. Thanks for including me in your expedition."

Of the eighty-nine dogs that sailed to Antarctica with Amundsen, only eleven survived the Norwegian's literal dog-eat-dog race to the South Pole. A one in nine survival rate is not great when you are talking about any animal in your care, but that is especially true if those animals are man's best friend. Imagine being on a baseball team, and everyone but the catcher dies, and then the catcher eats the first baseman. Actually, I think MLB would seriously consider this if they thought it would help the ratings. At the end of the day, those eleven surviving dogs were undoubtedly the most athletic and deeply disturbed canines to have ever set foot in Antarctica.

You Could Be A Friggin' Worm

You could be a worm. Normally, I try to be more specific when dunking on an animal but with very few exceptions I think it is fair to say that you are better off than basically all of the twenty-two thousand known species of worms. To be clear, when I say worms, I am speaking of segmented worms in the phylum **Annelida**, which is something I'm sure you were all wondering about. The words nerds out there may appreciate that the word "anus" comes from the Latin word for "ring" and so Annelida literally means "little anuses" or "little rings." This is in reference to the multiple body segments that define the members of this phylum. That being said, when I first read about that, all I pictured was a stack of assholes arranged side by side like a box of doughnuts.

If you would like to better picture a generic segmented worm, it is not hard. I want you to think about your human body and picture it naked. I know it is not pretty, what with the odd smelly bits hanging off here and there, randomly placed patches of hair, and bony limbs just sort of dangling about. Pay no attention to the awkwardness of your naked form and instead focus on your mouth. This disgusting, moist bundle of teeth and jowls leads down your esophagus, into your stomach, through your intestines, and ends at your butthole. Now imagine that this unbroken tube is your whole body. Just a disembodied mouth attached to a stretchy tube that passes food through it until it is pushed out the other side. Now fold a couple of organs into the meat, add all the body hair back onto the outside, and make it breathe through its skin. You have the basic body plan of a worm. Oh, and give each little section its own pair of ribs but make them out of fingernails instead of bones because worm "bones" are made of keratin.

Being a hairy intestine slithering its way through the earth is bad enough. But let's think about some of the pitfalls of being a defenseless, dirt-eating GI tract. Not being able to scream or cry makes it easy for people to ignore how fucked up it is to thread a fishing hook through your body and toss you into the water, where your fate is either very slowly drowning or being picked apart by panfish. Imagine if you pulled up to the pier, and the guy next to you pulled a kitten out of a Styrofoam tub and slid a barbed hook through its shoulder and tossed in the river. You would be horrified. After a few minutes the splashing stops, and the guy says "ahh, its dead. Time to rebait." He reels the lifeless corpse back in, tears it off the hook and repeats the process. Pretty messed up when it is something you can put a bow on, huh?

Scenario number two takes place in the garden. You and the kids are doing a bit of weeding and one of them pops a chunk of soil loose with a trowel, and there is a wriggling, bleeding bit of worm flagellating on the end of the shovel. What do you say? "Don't worry, kiddo, both of those ends will grow a new body! He'll be just fine."

That is technically true. An earth worm that is separated can survive and regenerate lost sections provided that one of its several hearts remains intact in each half. However, that analysis ignores that you just chopped something with a nervous system and pain receptors in half! Imagine how horrifying it would be from your perspective if a giant cut you in half at the waist and instead of apologizing or rendering aid, they just smiled and started lecturing their children on biology.

You Could Have Written A Detailed Description Of All The Symptoms Of A Fatal Snake Bite While Dying From That Snake Bite

These days it is not uncommon to see someone accidentally document their own death in pursuit of Internet fame, but what if you are recording yourself being unalived before **LiveLeaks** was created? Today anyone can film themselves going 110 mph on a motorcycle and being ripped in half when the **Prius** in front of them merges unexpectedly or livestreaming themselves cleaning a loaded handgun and making a mess on the ceiling, but in 1957 you had to do things a little differently.

Our hero's name is Dr. **Karl P. Schmidt**. Dr. Schimdt was a renowned expert in the field of reptile study working at the Chicago Field Museum. His story begins with the delivery of an unknown snake that was sent to his office by the Lincoln Park Zoo for identification. As Dr. Schmidt investigated the snake, he started to suspect that it was a **boomslang**. Besides having a very cool sounding name, the boomslang is a highly venomous snake native to Africa that possesses some interesting features. It is one of a handful of rear-fanged venomous snakes, which means that its fangs are located on the underside of its left and right ass cheeks, respectively. Nah, I'm kidding; its fangs are situated at the back of its mouth instead of the front, which is technically different but not *that* much different. Like, who gives a shit? Not me, certainly, but it is important to Dr. Schmidt's story. The boomslang also has unique venom in that it is a natural coagulant. It works by causing its victim's blood to form so many tiny clots that all its clotting factors are used up and the remaining blood gets very leaky. Without clotting agents, the boomslang's target will bleed to death as their body fluids seep through their mucus membranes and from the linings of blood vessels and organs. This is officially known as "not a good way to go."

Dr. Karl P. Schmidt (pictured above) doing what he loved, fucking with venomous snakes. This one is dead, the one that killed him was not.

Now if I knew anything about snakes and suspected that the one on my desk might be one of these boomslangs, I would put the lid back on the box and call it a day until I got some PPE and a raise. This was not so for Dr. Schmidt. In what would be later known as his "death diary," Dr. Schmidt wrote about being bitten by the boomslang.

"I was discussing the possibilities of it being a boomslang when I took it without thinking of any precaution, and it promptly bit me on the fleshy, lateral aspect of the left thumb…" That is a pretty amazing admission from a lauded snake expert. That would be like finding a cellphone that belonged to a bomb disposal tech in a crater, and his last text says "I'm like 90 percent sure this thing is going to explode at any moment. I'm going to kick it. LOL."

Apparently, Dr. Schmidt believed due to the young age of the snake and the shallow nature of the wound that the bite would not be fatal. He may have also believed as many did in that time that rear-fanged snakes were not effective at delivering venom into large prey because of how far back the fangs lay in the mouth. No matter the reason, old Schmitty decided not to seek treatment and instead decided to write down everything about the experience in order to create a list of the resulting symptoms and ailments that might arise. He hoped to turn his pain into the scientific community's gain. Instead, he left a grim and eerie timeline of worsening symptoms that ended with him being pronounced dead from respiratory failure less than a day after he was bitten.

Boomslang (Dispholidus typus) on a tree branch in Tanzania far away from careless herpetologist thumbs. Photo: William Warby

Some of the entries clearly showed the effects of venom such as, "5:30-6:30 strong chill and shaking followed by fever of 101.7 which did not persist. (Blankets and heating pad.)" "Bleeding in the mucus membranes of the mouth began at 5:30 apparently mostly at gums." "Urination at 12:20am mostly blood though small in amount. Mouth has bled steadily as shown by dried blood at both angles of the mouth." Some were quite anti-climactic, which is fair considering that he didn't know he was going to die. Still, the entry "8:30pm ate 2 pieces of milk toast" does not make for suspenseful reading. The diary of my last day will include many more references to cocaine rips and piles of hookers or possibly hugging my loved ones closely depending on who is reading this. (I love you, Sweetheart! I would never cheat on you with hookers! Kisses!)

At autopsy, it was revealed that Dr. Schmidt was bleeding from lots of places, not just his mouth and dick. Slightly more concerning than the bloody urine were all the clots they found in his brain, lungs, kidneys, intestines, eyes, heart, and stomach. The coroner concluded that death was caused by "cerebral hemorrhaging brought by snake bite envenomation." The cause of death could also have been accurately labeled "death by picking up a snake and then not being nearly worried enough when it bites you."

So, the next time you mess up at work just remember at least you didn't get killed by recklessly handling something you were supposed to have expert knowledge of, let alone something that even idiots know not to recklessly handle.

You Could Have Been Flash-Mummified While Rubbing One Out

You could forever be known as the "**masturbating man of Pompeii.**" The man in question is one of roughly 1000 people recovered from the buried ruins of Pompeii. You will recall that Pompeii was an ancient Roman town near the base of Mt. Vesuvius that was destroyed when the aforementioned volcano erupted in spectacular fashion in the year 79 AD.

The so-called "masturbating man of Pompeii" is one of many bodies that have been preserved in the moment of their death by the blanket of volcanic ash that entombed the entire town. This man is displayed at the site, lying on his back with his right hand very suggestively frozen in place over his crotch, his hand balled into a fist and holding something that may or may not be shaped exactly like a human penis.

To the casual immature onlooker, it looks very much like he was rubbing one out while fire and death rained down all around him, which is objectively awesome if true.

Just because his hand appears to be tightly grasping an object directly over his genital area, there is no evidence to suggest that this man has been preserved for all time in the middle of jerkin' his gherkin.

Despite the seemingly damning positioning, it is quite unfair to be characterized the way that he has been for a couple reasons.

Firstly, every guy in Pompeii was a **masturbating** man; they just didn't get flash mummified while doing it and then put on display in a glass case for all to see. Secondly, he probably wasn't actually cranking it to the impending apocalypse. Lame scientists in Italy have cast doubt on the possibility that he was playing pocket billiards inside his toga and instead claim that the extremely intense heat of the pyroclastic surge would have cooked the people of Pompeii instantly and caused their limbs to contract and curl into odd positions, such as, wrapping your hand perfectly around your genitals (Sure). Many of the other bodies at Pompeii seem to be contorted in cries of agony and writhing from the pain of being air fried but that is probably just the instant rigor mortis too right?

Just think, you may have been caught doing something embarrassing once or twice in your life. Picking your nose, waving at someone who wasn't waving at you, oogling your ex's bikini photos on her Instagram, or even playing a little game of "five on one" under the sheets. Take solace in the fact that you were not frozen in the middle of that mortifying action and subsequently displayed for all time in a museum.

You Could Have
Survived A Bullet And Gotten
Killed By A Finger

You could have been American President **James A. Garfield**. You may think his inclusion in this volume odd because usually you think of being president as something to aspire towards. This used to be true. That was before the Internet, DNA testing, the Freedom of Information Act, Twitter, and cellphone cameras ruined it. You would live in a mansion, fly in a private jet, get blown by interns without being caught (usually), order the occasional toppling of a foreign government for laughs and your table would get called first at the **Illuminati** sex buffet. Nowadays, the joy of smuggling prostitutes in and out of the Oval Office has been lost to twenty-four-hour news coverage and anonymous sources in the Secret Service. Fortunately for President Jimmy G., he lived in a simpler time when presidents didn't use security. There were no bodyguards ruining the mood at their orgies or spoiling a good "darkie joke" (Abe Lincoln's words not mine, don't cancel me). Unfortunately for Garfield, he lived in a simpler time when Presidents didn't use security.

So it was that when **Charles Guiteau** stepped behind the President on July 2, 1881, and pressed a revolver to his back, there were no bodyguards there to stop him from pulling the trigger. Guiteau shot the president twice while they were standing in the lobby of the Baltimore and Potomac Railroad Station. Garfield was taken conscious, but in shock, back to the White House to await what was expected to be his death.

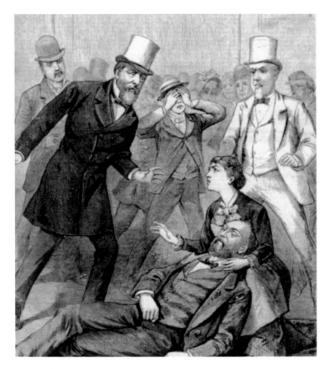

Artist's rendition of scene immediately following President Garfield being shot. The President has collapsed and is attended to by those in crowd. Colonel Sanders (back right) looks on and asks if fried chicken can somehow improve the situation.

Luckily for Garfield, his assassin had no idea about what he was doing. Guiteau had no prior experience with firearms and only chose the particular gun that he used because he felt that ivory grips would look better in a museum exhibit than those made of wood. His shot placement was terrible with one bullet grazing the president's shoulder and the other lodging itself next to his backbone without piercing it or any of the other important stuff floating around in there.

Unluckily for Garfield, the doctors of his day also had no idea what they were doing. Not only were they wrong on the initial prognosis of the president not surviving the night, but they were also wrong about nearly everything else they did.

President Garfield would live for seventy-nine agonizing days after he was shot. Rather than trauma from the initial wound, it was the subsequent infections he sustained that eventually killed him. Several doctors repeatedly examined the president and dug around in his now pus-filled bullet wound with their dirty, gloveless, bacteria-covered hands because at that time most doctors still believed that hand washing was not necessary. The general consensus seemed to be, "Hog wash! Just because everyone I have put my hands inside of dies from infection does not mean there is a correlation. We simply haven't given them enough cocaine and tobacco syrup."

Besides the small setback of not knowing what bacteria are, President Garfield's treatment was actually impressive for its technological advancement in several ways (not that it made any difference). For instance, army engineers created a rudimentary, first-of-its-kind air conditioning unit for the president's room consisting of a series of fans, ductwork and massive blocks of ice. This impressive contraption managed to lower the room's temperature by twenty degrees, which helped ease the vicious fevers that would take hold of Garfield due to all the finger dirt in his abdomen.

Additionally, famed inventor **Alexander Graham Bell** developed a metal detector to try and locate the bullet and used it, albeit unsuccessfully. Though the device did work, the president's metal bed frame caused false readings. Even without this setback the metal detector would have failed. This is because Garfield's chief doctor wrongly believed the bullet to be on the right side of Garfield's torso when in fact it was on the left side where Bell was forbidden to look for some perplexing reason.

The doctor's erroneous belief that the bullet had gone hither when in fact it had turned thither led to those grimy fingers creating a completely new and unnecessary wound tract on the wrong side of the body. One of the doctors even ruptured Garfield's liver while rooting around in there.

Death graciously saved President Garfield on September 19, 1881, more than eleven weeks after his shooting. His autopsy revealed that he had advanced sepsis and pus-filled abscesses throughout his body, which I'm sure were attributed to "bullets just sort of doing that to people if you leave them in there too long." The bullet itself was encased in a sort of cyst that would have likely prevented lead poisoning or other contamination of the wound. In fact, many subsequent analyses have suggested that because the bullet didn't actually hit anything crucial and had been naturally encased by Garfield's immune system, he almost certainly would have lived if not for those disgusting, ass-picking, booger-flicking, funked- up phalanges rifling around in his pistol wound. The president of the United States was likely killed not by an assassin's bullet but by his own doctor's dirty-ass hands.

A Sitting U.S. President
Could Have Died Every Time
The Two Of You Were
In a Room Together

Robert Todd Lincoln holds the unenviable record for being present for the most presidential assassinations in history (sort of). Have you ever been watching a sporting event, and every time you came into the room something bad happened to your team? Were you then banished to the backyard for the remainder of the game by your superstitious friends and family? Did you impose the sentence on yourself for the sake of the [who gives a shit team's name]? Well, something like this happened to Robert Todd Lincoln (sort of).

Once whereupon being invited to a White House event, he allegedly remarked, "If only they knew, they wouldn't want me there. There is a certain fatality about presidential functions when I am present."

Why would he utter such a thing? Well, Robert Todd Lincoln was the son of President **Abraham Lincoln**. The same President Abraham Lincoln who was assassinated at the Ford's Theatre on April 14, 1865. The younger Lincoln was not actually present when his dad was Sic Semper Tyrannis'ed but he was by his father's side when President Lincoln died the next morning.

Robert Todd Lincoln pictured in between seeing his first and second assassinations. Present but not visible is the aura of presidential death that seeped from his pores.

Robert Lincoln (now serving as secretary of war) was present six-teen years later when President Garfield was shot. He witnessed the event as he was approaching President Garfield in the train station lobby where Robert planned to see the president off. As secretary of war, Robert ordered troops to secure the White House (in those days you could pretty much just walk right up to the president's house which is fucking bonkers) and the prison where Charles Guiteau was being held so that he would not be lynched. Robert would visit the ailing President at least once before his death. Lincoln and the rest of the cabinet met Garfield in one of the brief moments that someone wasn't tunneling around in his bloated abdomen.

Twenty years later, Robert Todd Lincoln was on his way to the Pan-American exposition in Buffalo, New York when he was handed a letter informing him that another visitor of the exhibition had just been shot. That person was none other than twenty-sixth president **William McKinley.** The now private citizen Robert Lincoln, who was now 0-2 in seeing recovering-assassination-attempt-victims survive, visited the wounded President McKinley to see if he could bag himself an assassination hat trick. Robert visited the president twice and was confident that McKinley would recover, later writing that "My visit has given me much encouragement [as to the survival of the president]". Eight days later President McKinley was dead, so I guess don't ask old Bert to tell you how sick you are.

While it is not true that Robert Todd Lincoln was present for three presidential assassinations, he did visit three presidents on their deathbeds which is enough for any man to start wondering… …maybe it's me? While it is debated whether Robert actually swore off being around American Presidents after Mckinley's death you could hardly blame him for avoiding them. Honestly, I think they probably just stopped inviting him to things to keep the bodies from piling up at his ankles.

If I were commander-in-chief and somebody handed me a guest list with Robert Todd Lincoln's name on it, I wouldn't have to think twice about it. "Are you kidding me? Mr. Bhlam-O-McShooty-bad-omen-never-come-near-me-in-a-hospital-bed-or-otherwise himself? No. Tear that thing up and cancel the event and hang yourself for treason. Not today buddy!"

Also, I know this last one is a stretch, but the last time he was with another United States president was when Robert was present for the dedication of the Lincoln Memorial in 1922. He was invited by **President Warren G. Harding** who stood with him at the monument. President Harding would die suddenly in office fourteen months later from congestive heart failure presumably shouting for someone to lock his bedroom door lest Robert Todd Lincoln come bouncing in with a cloud of presidential death hanging over him.

You Could Have Been A Retired George Washington And Get A Cold Before We Knew The Difference Between Torture And Medicine

Nowadays a cold means that you get to call off work and daydream about how screwed Lindsey and the rest of the girls are gonna be when the dinner rush hits at Applebee's. In basically all of human history before yesterday, it meant that you would have to see a doctor and he was going to do something awful to you in the name of "medicine".

*Portrait of **George Washington**, father of a nation, commander of the Continental Army, first president of The United States of America and known cherry tree vandalizer He is pictured here in 1795, Four years before his death was assisted by, if not flat out caused by whack-a-do "medical treatments".*

The year was 1799 and the first president of the United States had woken suddenly around 2 a.m. to a painfully swollen throat. He woke his wife Martha and informed her of his affliction. Martha roused one of their slaves. (Yes, they had slaves; don't let it distract you. It's not important. I mean, it is hugely important but not to this story, so let's gloss over it like my school curriculum did.) Anyway, the slaves woke Washington's secretary Tobias Lear. Tobias woke farm overseer George Rawlins who woke a doctor and friend of Washington named Dr. James Craik. That's a lot of people getting woken up in the middle of the damn night for a man with a sore throat. That should give you an indication of how bad your chances were against the flu back in those days. When Rawlins arrived with the others at the former president's bed, Washington asked the overseer to bleed him.

For the uninitiated, "bleeding" is a cuckoo-for-cocoa-puffs "medical" procedure that was used to treat many unrelated diseases and afflictions thought to be caused by an imbalance of one or more of the four humors of the body (blood, phlegm, yellow bile and black bile). This completely bullshit theory originated in the fourth century BC in ancient Greece and wasn't fully debunked until the late 1800's which means… … holy shit humans were dumb for a really long time. Anywhoo, Washington wanted to be bled in the hopes that removing some of his blood would take his inflammation down. If you are swollen, it was thought you must have too much blood. Take some out, and the swelling will go down.

Overseer Rawlins was happy to oblige and opened up the retired general's arm and let out about a cup of blood while they waited for Dr. Craik. Washington's attendants also gave him a mix of butter, molasses, and vinegar, which was supposed to soothe his aching throat. This only managed to nearly suffocate him as the thick, sticky concoction was very difficult to swallow through his badly swollen throat. Go figure. Once Dr. Craik arrived, he bled Georgie for the second time and ordered a vinegar and sage tea to be prepared to help with the sore throat, which I'm sure helped immensely. Nothing sounds more soothing than treating a sore throat with hot, acidic, vinegar tea. Dr. Craik then sent for a second doctor, who arrived the following morning and administered another absurd but very common treatment of the day called **blistering**.

Blistering was the practice of burning or using chemical agents to raise a blister on the patient's skin over the area closest to whatever organ that was believed to be afflicted. The rationale behind doing so was that the fluid that filled the blister could be drained and in doing so, further help to lower inflammation. In Washington's case this was done by applying a compound taken from a beetle known as "Spanish fly" to his throat. For those keeping track, the "Father of America" has now had butter, vinegar, molasses, sage, and caustic beetle juices smeared on or poured down his severely swollen and irritated throat in addition to being drained of a significant portion of his blood. When Washington's condition did not improve, a third doctor was dispatched and somewhere in between he was given an enema, bled a third time, and given various other bogus home remedies. Once the third doctor arrived, they decided to really lean into the blood-letting and drained an additional thirty-two ounces from what I can imagine was a rather pale looking Washington.

For good measure they decided to give him something to induce vomiting, which also did not help because why the fuck would that help? At this point, Washington was pretty certain that he was going to die or perhaps he was just hoping to die so people would stop burning him and draining his blood off. Either way, he asked that Martha bring him his will and gave instructions on the affairs of his estate to Rawlins and Lear. For some reason, even though everybody had basically confirmed Washington's fate, they still insisted on blistering him more. This time they chemically burned his legs and feet, presumably because it was the only part of him they hadn't mutilated yet.

After his final "treatment", Washington rose from his bed, dressed himself, and being ever the gentleman, thanked each doctor individually for mutilating/treating him and returned to bed. He died two hours later on December 14, 1799.

So in review, at the request of the first president and under the direction of 3 medical doctors, eighty ounces (40 percent) of Washington's blood was drained over the course of twelve hours; his throat, legs, and feet were burned and cut open; and various hokey home remedies were shoved down his throat and up his ass to absolutely zero positive effect before he finally, thankfully, died at age sixty-seven. To this day no one knows what killed George Washington (apart from his doctors), but what *is* known is that medicine for basically all of human history was a nightmare.

You Could Have Contracted Just About Every Illness Known To Man While Running A Country

You could have been George Washington at pretty much any other point in life when he wasn't feeling good. In his sixty-seven years, Washington would contract and survive mumps, measles, diphtheria, tuberculosis, smallpox, influenza, pneumonia, dysentery, malaria and possibly mouth cancer. He would develop serious arthritis in his arms, become almost completely deaf, and lose all but one of his teeth by the time he died. Almost all of his afflictions were treated with some crazy-ass ineffective or straight up toxic mix of herbs and heavy metals and almost always accompanied by blood-letting because the past was horrible.

The next time you get the runs after trying a new food truck and have to suffer through work the next day, be glad that you aren't battling at least five different incurable diseases at once while running a fledgling nation.

You Could Be The Dumbest Looking, Most Awkward, Flea-Bitten Abomination In The Ocean

You could be a mola mola. The mola mola is also known as ocean sunfish and also also known as the dumbest looking creature in the ocean. The English common name of "ocean sunfish" is actually one of the nicer names given to this unfortunate, frumpy, wrinkled, oversized frisbee of a fish. Here is a small list of some of translated names for the mola from around the world: Finnish: Lump fish; German: swimming head; Polish: head only, head alone; Chinese: toppled wheel head; and globally: -stupid-dumb-dinner-plate-looking-dick-munch fish. The reason so many countries have names for the mola is that it can be found in all of the world's oceans.

Readers will recall the ocean as the home to ninety percent of the animals you would least like to be reincarnated as, and the mola is no exception. Besides looking like it was drawn by a child who has never actually seen a fish, the mola holds the record for harboring the most numerous and varied catalogue of parasites in the animal kingdom. Over forty different species of parasite regularly call this fish home/dinner. In fact, its English name of "Sunfish" comes from its habit of "sunning" itself on its side on the surface of the water. This is apparently done to invite seagulls to help rid it of parasites. This is a bit of a mixed bag though, because the gulls sometimes just start picking at the flesh of the mola instead of cleaning it.

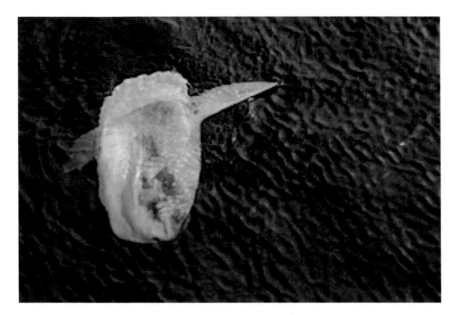

A mola swims on its side near the surface, practicing the same behavior that earned the mola its nickname, the sunfish. The mola perfectly mimics the Sun's characteristic dead-looking skin, vacant, idiotic mouth and floppy, sail-like fins. Photo: National Marine Sanctuaries/NCAA

Getting back down from the surface can be tricky too because the mola does not come standard with a swim bladder, which is how most fish orient themselves right side up in the water. Swim bladders also keep other fish from sinking when they stop swimming, so it kind of seems like a weird thing to not have. Because they lack the swim bladder, it is not uncommon to see molas swimming sideways in strong currents. Scientists used to think that molas could not swim at all and were basically only able to sort of steer wherever they were being carried. This shows just how worthless scientists are because not only can molas swim, but they can apparently get up enough speed to jump out of the water.

This is definitely the most impressive thing this stupid fish can do because it means that although they lack teeth, or really any weapons, they have actually managed to kill at least one person before. This reportedly happened when a mola breached and landed on top of a small boat, crushing and killing one of the occupants. Yeah, when I said they were big I wasn't kidding. Molas typically grow to 6 ft long, 8 ft tall, and weigh around 2200 lbs. with the world record-holding mola weighing over 5000 lbs. when caught.

Just like humans, it seems that the animals who have the least business procreating often do it the most, and so it is with the mola. It is estimated that the mola releases as many as three hundred million eggs at a times. This ludicrous number of offspring ensures that no matter how worthless these idiots are, at least a couple of the ridiculous critters make it to adulthood. So, to sum it up, mola molas are ugly ugly, badly designed, and somehow incredibly prolific. They are basically the PT Cruisers of the sea.

You Could Be a Fish Sealed In A Mucus Condom Under A Dried-Up River Bed In The Desert

You could be an African **Lungfish**. Whereas the mola appears out of place in the water because it doesn't look like a fish, the lungfish looks out of place because it is a fish. Specifically, it is because you can often find lungfish hanging out in the middle of the desert.

Lungfish are fish. They live in rivers However, those rivers are in sub-Saharan Africa. Every summer it gets very hot, and the lack of rain makes the rivers dry up. For most fish, running out of water is what biologists call "a problem." Lungfish are not bothered by this minor setback though, because they have something that other fish don't: A specialized swim bladder surrounded by bundles of tiny blood vessels that help to pull oxygen out of the air which the lungfish swallows. You thought I was going to say lungs, didn't you? Well, that's why I write the books, and you read them while on the toilet.

Using this adaptation, the lungfish can gulp air from the surface rather than rely on the increasingly oxygen-deficient and rapidly evaporating water when the dry season rolls around.

When the water level drops below a certain point, the lungfish abandons the surface and begins to burrow straight down into the mud below. Some researchers believe that the lungfish are attempting to burrow through the Earth until they reach the other side. Further research has shown that this is patently absurd because the Earth is flat and tunneling through it would land you in the vacuum of space. In reality, lungfish embed themselves in the mud and begin a process known by nerds as aestivation.

An illustration of a lungfish in all its various phases. Slithering around on the riverbed, getting fat enough to play dead (top), making a booger coffin and just sort of staring at the wall (bottom right), and being basically dead while getting turned into a fish raisin and waiting for some rain (bottom left).

During aestivation, the lungfish greatly diminishes its metabolic rate and becomes dormant. It will then secrete a thick layer of mucus that will harden from the outside as the riverbed dries out. Imagine tucking yourself into bed by rubbing snot over yourself until you have a full-body booger sleeping bag. Now imagine just sort of holding your breath and counting to one hundred... ...days.

The lungfish will remain in its mucus mattress for as long as the ground is dry, with the longest heat hiatus lasting two years in a laboratory setting.

"How was college?"

"Well, I spent two years looking at a fish my professor mummified."

"Because it could hold the secret to curing cancer?"

"No, I think just for the hell of it, you know?"

While dormant, the lungfish sustains itself by playing "I spy with my little eye something mud-colored" with itself and digests its own muscle tissues for nutrients. You would think that spending half your life in a you-shaped hole in the mud, holding your pee, and eating yourself would leave you wanting to party a little bit during the rainy season, but that's not how the lungfish rolls. Because of their half-assed breathing apparatus and need to conserve energy for the ever-looming snot nap, lungfish are largely inactive. They spend most of their time on the riverbed, munching on whatever floats by, and rising only to breathe every thirty minutes or so. By conserving every spare calorie through utter laziness, the lungfish can ensure that it has enough energy to survive its annual dehydration. So, the lungfish spends half its time being barely alive so it can afford to be basically dead for the rest of the year.

West African lungfish (Protopterus annectens) displaying its most ambitious behavior: laying very still at the bottom of a river in preparation for lying very still under the bottom of the river. Real party animal this one...

You Could Have Learned The Sticky Side Of Gender Equality While Your Ship Was Sinking In Freezing Waters

You could have been the passengers of the **SS Arctic** when it sank off the coast of Newfoundland. Now being on any ship that is sinking is not going to be a good time, but the poor bastards that found themselves going for an impromptu dip in the North Atlantic on September 27, 1854, had a few more reasons to be unhappy with their situation than the average human buoy. Especially if they were any of the women and children, all of whom died during the wreck.

The SS Arctic was a passenger steam ship powered by two large paddles on either side of her hull. She was considered fast for her day and could make fifteen **knots** in good conditions. The Arctic was crewed by 153, and on the day she sank she had an additional 250 passengers on board. The Arctic was sailing under two conditions that contributed to the severity of the disaster.

The first was common for her day and that was that she had only six lifeboats, with enough capacity for less than half of those on board. Sounds pretty stupid, and it is, but you know you live and you learn… or you don't and it continues to cause excess death in pretty much every shipwreck for the next fifty-eight years until a little dinghy called the RMS Titanic goes down in pretty much the same place as the Arctic and it makes a big enough splash (don't excuse the pun) that Congress gets involved.

The second condition was less common, and it was that the owners and financiers of the Arctic insisted that she maintain her top speed regardless of the situation in order to maintain her tight schedule.

The Arctic was a paddleboat much like the small, foot pedal-powered boat you can rent at water parks as a kid. Except the Arctic was much larger and steam powered and at the end of the ride the kids didn't get off.

On the morning of her sinking, the Arctic was passing through dense fog at full speed when a lookout spotted another ship headed straight for them. Captain James Luce ordered the Arctic to zig when he should have zagged (as is customary in maritime navigation). This led to the other ship, the SS Vesta, ramming the front of Arctic. The Vesta was an iron-hulled French fishing vessel with a nifty **bowsprit** protruding from the front of her hull. This long pole is used to pierce the sides of other ships and skewer any hapless sailor who is standing in the way. Well, technically bowsprits aren't actually made for that, but that is what happened in this case.

The Arctic was still moving along, and its much larger size meant that it tore the entire bow off the front of the Vesta before the two finally dislodged from each other. Except for those on deck, barely anyone inside the Arctic realized there'd been a collision (except for the guy who got shish kabobbed; I'm pretty sure he knew something was wrong). Onboard the Vesta, however, the entire ship was thrown into chaos. The front half of the ship was quickly dipping lower into the ocean as water rushed into the gaping hole in the front, and sailors were desperately clambering to the back of the ship. Captain Luce immediately ordered that two of the Arctic's lifeboats be lowered and sent to help with the evacuation of the Vesta. However, only one of these boats made it to the water before Luce called it back. Luce noticed that the massive paddle wheels that propelled the ship sounded more labored than usual and guessed that the ship must be sitting lower in the water. He ordered the Arctic to be reexamined and a more thorough inspection revealed that there were two large holes below the waterline and that the ship was indeed taking on water. When the crew went below to try to plug the holes, they found that this section of the ship was too far below the water to work on. Unless they could reach land, the Arctic was going to sink.

Having lost sight of their first lifeboat and knowing that time was of the essence, Captain Luce ordered the Arctic to abandon the lifeboat crew and the sinking Vesta and make for Newfoundland. This order came as very unwelcome news to the lifeboat full of French sailors pulling up alongside the Arctic. They had just finished rowing away from the Vesta and into what they thought was their rescue when the Arctic's paddles roared to life again. Before anything could be done, the entire lifeboat was smashed against the paddle and all but one of the occupants was mangled in the churning paddles and killed.

This unfortunate accident is made even more tragic by the fact that if those men had just stayed with the Vesta they all would have lived. That's right; the Vesta did not sink. Unlike the wooden-hulled Arctic, the Vesta had four watertight bulkheads, and because the damage and sea water was contained to the forward bulkhead, the Vesta was able to safely limp into port. Those onboard the Vesta did not learn the fate of the Arctic until survivors started trickling in.

Back onboard the Arctic, the scene was rapidly degenerating. Seawater eventually reached the boiler fires and extinguished them. With no more steam power to move the paddles, the fate of the Arctic was sealed. Captain Luce ordered the remaining lifeboats to be launched, with the women and children getting priority. The first of these boats (second boat to launch) was loaded, provisioned, and put under the command of the ship's butcher. He was ordered to stay by the Arctic's side so that all the boats could proceed to land together. This was a good idea, so naturally it was ignored. The butcher and the only one of the Arctic's lifeboats that was fully loaded drifted off and was never recovered. Presumably because they sent a butcher instead of a sailor to pilot it.

The third boat was being loaded with women and children as well, when a group of crewmen pushed past the crowd and jumped into the lifeboat in an effort to save themselves. This caused the lifeboat to break free of its winch, dumping all the occupants into the sea. Although some of the men who jumped did survive, all the women and children who fell into the sea drowned.

This third lifeboat was refloated. (I didn't know you could refloat a boat… don't know why they didn't do that to the Arctic; could have saved a lot of headache.) It was then loaded with-you guessed it- another bunch of dudes who courageously pushed the women and children aside in order to save themselves.

The fourth lifeboat was put under the command of the second mate, a man named Balhaam. This boat was rushed by the crew, and when it floated away half full, only a single passenger was among them. That passenger was of course, a dude. Captain Luce ordered Balhaam to remain by the Arctic and pick up those in the water, but in keeping with the theme of the day, Balhaam immediately disregarded the captain and rowed away. There were now only two lifeboats remaining.

The fifth boat was being hijacked by the ship's engine staff while everyone else was busy being terrible to one another on the other side of the ship. The chief engineer told anyone who questioned their motives that this boat was being prepared to go alongside the Arctic to attempt more repairs. In reality, the engineers simply absconded with the lifeboat.

The sixth and final lifeboat was lowered into the water without its paddles so that no one would be tempted to steal it, and used to make a bridge on which a makeshift raft was built. The remaining passengers tore apart everything they could that would float and began tying it together. As the deck of the Arctic got closer and closer to the waterline, panic overcame the remaining passengers and they rushed the final lifeboat, breaking it free without its oars and plunging the raft it was supporting into the water.

With nothing left for anyone to steal a spot on, the few crewmembers left and most of the passengers huddled together and prayed, resigning themselves to dying with grace. Just kidding it was fucking anarchy. The remaining men raided the liquor stores, forced themselves on women, fought each other, and spread general chaos.

Captain Luce gathered his eleven-year-old partially disabled son from his quarters and held him closely at his post atop the starboard paddle box. When the ship went down the two of them disappeared below the surface in the suction created by the massive ship along with most of the passengers still aboard. Captain Luce and his boy actually managed to reach the surface again, but when the paddle box they had been standing on ripped free from the ship, it rose with such force that it killed Luce's boy and several others upon striking them. Captain Luce would survive along with eighty-eight of those aboard the Arctic. Of those, only twenty-four were passengers, and all were adult males.

An artist's rendition of the sinking of the SS Arctic. Visible in the drawing is the bullshit raft made of timbers, and the lifeboats that are filled with dudes who are presumably pretending that they can't hear the hopeless wails of all the women and children they abandoned.

Tragedy was certain the moment that the Vesta collided with the Arctic but much of the death and suffering could have been avoided. If everyone had listened to Captain Luce, it is likely that twice that number of people could have survived. Only one lifeboat was actually filled to capacity, and half of the boats were lost at sea along with all of their occupants. The panic that caused this misappropriation was unnecessary because the relatively slow speed at which the Arctic sank left plenty of time for the evacuation of those on board. The most valuable thing to take away from this lesson in selfishness, arrogance, and incompetence is that you should never go on a cruise, ever.

You Could've Drowned
In A Festering Pool
Of Human Waste
And Industrial Sludge

Slowly dying in frigid waters as the result of a shipwreck is a shitty way to go, but not literally a shitty way to go. That is not the case for the next group of involuntary swimmers. You could have been onboard the **SS Princess Alice** when it sank directly in the middle of seventy-five million gallons of raw sewage.

The scene was **London, England** and the SS Princess Alice was on the moonlight run of its passenger-ferrying service on the Thames River. At around the halfway point of the return trip to London, the Princess Alice made a maneuver to avoid the SS Bywell Castle. This coal-carrying ship was not much longer than the Princess Alice, but it was nearly four times her weight. Using math, you can therefore calculate that when the two massive objects collided, the Princess Alice was completely screwed. It is possible that the helmsman of the Princess Alice underestimated the speed that the Bywell Castle was travelling at, or he may have overestimated the speed at which the Princess Alice could turn. Either way, it is hard to blame him for his ignorance seeing as he was not actually part of the crew.

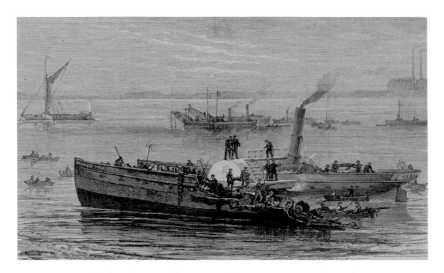

Men remove bodies from the front half of the SS Princess Alice after the deadly collision. Gotta say, even without the broken ship covered in bodies. The Thames River in the industrial revolution looks like a disaster.

I'm not kidding. Apparently, the actual helmsman for the Princess Alice wanted to get off at the previous stop and the captain agreed and replaced him with a random dickhead from the passenger body. This man had no experience with paddle ships and had not piloted on the Thames before but was a sailor by trade, which is apparently enough credentials to steer a boat with nine-hundred people onboard in the dark. Unsurprisingly, Princess Alice did not make it across the bow of the Bywell Castle in time. As the collision was imminent the captain of the Bywell was heard shouting "Where are you coming to? Good God, where are you coming to?!"

Everyone else onboard the Bywell was probably shouting, "Way to go you moron! What, is it your first time piloting a paddle ship on an unfamiliar river at night?" To which the mystery helmsman replied with,

"AHHHHH!!!" because at that moment, the Bywell smashed into the starboard side of the Princess Alice, ripping her in two instantaneously. The Princess Alice sank so quickly that all but two of the people below deck drowned before they could escape.

Those trapped below may have actually been the lucky ones, though because the spot at which the deadly collision happened was immediately next to the pumping station for all of London's sewage. Firmly in the middle of the **industrial age**, human waste might have been the least offensive thing running through London's sewers. The sludge being deposited into the Thames was a toxic mix of industrial runoff, solvents, tars, dyes, slaughterhouse byproducts, fertilizers, ash, and every manner of garbage. A chemist would later describe the sewage effluent as "Two continuous columns of decomposed, fermenting sewage, hissing like soda-water with baneful gases, so black that the water is stained for miles and discharging a corrupt charnel-house odor…"

This disgusting sewage would normally just harmlessly pollute the riverbed and make all the wildlife do tricks like floating upside down and melting, but now there was a different type of wildlife being slimed to death… **tourists**. Onlookers described the horror as hundreds of people, stained black by the polluted water, weighed down by their heavy clothing, and blinded by poisonous ooze, all drowned within minutes of the sinking. Many people were rendered unconscious by the fumes and others could not break the surface of the thick sludge and dense mass of bodies.

The toxic mixture was so polluted that sixteen people who survived the initial incident died from infections, and many more would fall seriously ill from their contact with the filth. Despite an outpouring of aid from witnesses on the banks and several responding ships, an estimated 650-750 people died. Their bodies quickly bloated from the septic sludge, and identifying them was nearly impossible. The recovery efforts took weeks as decomposing tourists were found washed up on the shores of the Thames for miles downstream.

A crowd gathers at the Woolrich Dockyard to identify the bodies of victims pulled from the wreck of The Princess Alice. Nothing says 1800's England quite like getting dressed in your Sunday finest so you can bring your kids down to the docks to look at a bunch of bloated, shit-covered corpses.

The outrage from the horrific scene led to major reforms in the prevalent sanitation and waste disposal methods of the day, which led to the end of sewer dumping in the river. Instead, sewer barges were constructed to remove the effluent. These ships carried the putrid waste of the city out to sea and dumped it there, where it couldn't harm anyone… except for all the fish, whales, dolphins, sharks, crabs, shrimp, seals, sea gulls, albatrosses, krill, plankton, algae, jellyfish, sea stars, urchins, squids, lobsters, octopuses, orcas, oysters, and everything else living there. The practice of dumping London's waste at sea would continue until -Holy steaming people shit- 1998?! Is that true? Goddamn it, it is true. Honestly, letting the river even the score with a few hundred Britons is the least they could do.

You Could Have Been Treading Water For Three Days Straight With About A Thousand Sharks

Speaking of shipwrecks made infinitely worse by the things that are in the water when you go down, you could have been among the crew of the **U.S.S. Indianapolis** when it was torpedoed in the South Pacific on July 31, 1945. The Indianapolis had just finished delivering a new kind of powerful microwave oven that could instantly cook any meal within a ten-mile radius of where it was used. This revolutionary culinary device was delivered to an airbase in the Marianas Islands, where it would be assembled and gifted to the people of Japan. Twice. (I'm talking about the atom bombs for any special eddies who have made it this far. For the rest of you, this is about the darkest the humor is going to get so bear with me. It's all up from here.)

On the Indianapolis's return trip, somewhere between Guam and San Fransisco, a Japanese submarine scored two critical hits (no word on bonus xp) on the Indianapolis, sinking her in twelve minutes. Of the twelve hundred men onboard, about nine hundred survived the initial sinking. They clung to a few life rafts, and various pieces of debris and waited for rescue. By the time that rescue came almost four days later, there were only 317 men left alive.

*The USS Indianapolis pictured in 1939. The only thing worse than being trapped on a giant metal boat in the middle of the ocean with a thousand other dudes during wartime would be suddenly, and violently **not** being trapped in a giant metal boat in the middle of the ocean during wartime with a thousand man-eating sharks.*

The things in the water that I poorly foreshadowed earlier were sharks, and they were quickly drawn in by the chaos of the wreck. At first the sharks feasted on the many dead, but gradually they became more confident and started feeding on the living. Men huddled together and tried to defend themselves in shifts, but the sharks were relentless. The lack of drinkable water and shade led to many men fainting and drifting off to be fed upon. Days of waiting with no rest, food, or water was a hellish ordeal punctuated by the screams of the unlucky souls being thrashed by the sharks. By the time the last seaman was pulled from the water, sharks had killed twice as many men as the Japanese sub had. That means that in a surprise attack, the Japanese sub crew placed second in a battle in which they fired the only shots and lost zero men. (third if you count the after-kills when the bomb the Indianapolis delivered went off in Hiroshima.)

You Could Have Played A Game Of Red Rover Except One Side Was People And The Other Side Was A Shit-Load Of Saltwater Crocodiles

If Oceanic white-tip sharks are on team Axis, then saltwater crocodiles definitely belong on team Allies. It is for this reason that you would not want to be a Japanese soldier during the **Battle of Ramree Island** on February 1, 1945.

When British troops encircled a group of around one thousand Japanese defenders, they repeatedly called for the latter to surrender. The Japanese soldiers refused, citing a centuries-old tradition of not giving up a fight until you get nuked at least twice. Instead, they retreated into a mangrove swamp, hoping to cross the nearly ten-mile gap between themselves and the main force on the other side.

Nearly half of these soldiers would die in the coming days, succumbing to dehydration, malaria, and the nearly always fatal condition of being torn to shreds by crocodiles. British soldiers patrolling the edges of the swamp reported terrible screams and gunfire throughout the night, and locals would later report at least one incident of 10-15 soldiers being eaten by frenzied crocs as they attempted to cross a tidal stream. The incident has been called the largest single crocodile attack in history. There are a number of disputes as to how many soldiers were actually killed by the crocs as opposed to being eaten after death, which is a very historian-y thing to argue about. One thing that is not in dispute is how a painting of the event would make the most metal album cover ever.

Of course, there are some wet blankets out there that have tried to disprove the numbers and in fact the reported numbers of around 500-900 dead do seem suspiciously high. What is more suspicious to me is how the **Ramree massacre** (as it is called) can actually be described as a mass crocodile "attack". If a KFC bucket opened your front door and plopped down on your TV tray at dinnertime, you wouldn't say that you went out of your way to "attack" those chicken thighs, now would you? Likewise, if I'm a 20 ft. long apex predator and I wake up to the sound of "For the love of God, surrender! Going in that jungle is suicide; you'll surely be torn apart by crocs!" And then the other guy says,

"Eat my shorts limey! I'd rather die!" I would take that as an invitation to start eating.

We will never know how many Japanese soldiers died in the Ramree swamps, but since saltwater crocodiles have been known to live to over a hundred years old, there is probably at least one saltie out there that knows what a Japanese soldier in uniform tastes like.

You Could Be The Dumbest Looking Reptile In The World And That's Saying Something

You could have been a snake that looks like a sock puppet. Whether it is looking badass slithering out of the eye-hole of a skull tattoo or looking badass as the physical representation of Satan in the Bible, most snakes enjoy a rather dangerous and fearsome image. All snakes except the **Arabian sand boa,** that is. Instead of an awesome killing machine, the Arabian sand boa looks like Kermit the frog got reimagined as a snake with Downs Syndrome. The Arabian sand boa's face looks like it was drawn by a kindergartener who should be ashamed of his work. Why does this unfortunate-looking reptile have such a permanently derpy expression? Well, it has to do with the way it hunts.

Arabian sand boas have their beady little upward facing eyes perched high on their heads so that when they bury themselves in the sand while waiting for prey, they can still see dinner coming. Being buried in hot-ass desert sand with nothing but my eyeballs hanging out there getting sunburned, and windblown seems like a steep price for a good view, but what are they going to do; hunt at night when only 90 percent of all desert creatures are active?

Do you know how many overcast days there are in the desert? Zero. Zero also happens to be the number of eyelids that sand boas have. This means

that while the scorching sun stares down on the sand boa's unblinking eyes, those misshapen, googly-eyes stare right back up at it. And when the prey comes, then what? The sand boa strikes at the perfect moment, lunging like a scaly muppet from the sand, when there is a zero percent chance that it doesn't catch a mouthful of sand every time. You know when you have a picnic on the beach and every time you take a bite of your soggy PB&J sandwich you can feel the gritty sand granules just grinding down your tooth enamel? That is Bug-Eye McBoa's daily routine. Not only is it the dumbest looking, least intimidating-snake to ever slither the cursed ground, but it must do so with a silhouette of the sun etched into its dead-looking eyes and sand in its teeth with no water to gargle it out with.

You Could Have Your Genitals Cut Off By A Fucking Mind-Controlling Barnacle

This is an all-too-common fate of the European green crab. If you have ever been to Memphis, Tennessee then you know how much it sucks to have an **STD**. (That's not me; that's according to 2022 statistics that show that Memphis has the highest STD rate per a hundred thousand people.) Anyway, what if you could catch an STD without even having sex or doing a bit of harmless needle sharing? So it is for a large percentage of green crabs.

The STD in question is not a virus or bacterial infection and technically isn't really an STD but a parasite known as the **castrator barnacle**. This ruthless little bastard **barnacle** starts life, as all barnacles do, by floating around as a tiny, free-swimming larva. At some point this larva finds an unsuspecting host crab and squeezes through the crab's shell. Once inside, the larva transforms, putting out rootlike tendrils that dig into various organs of the host crab and start to do pretty awful stuff. The first thing is getting into position. The castrator barnacle needs to set up shop somewhere out of the way of those pinching claws, and the perfect spot seems to be right where the crab's genitals are supposed to be*. The castrator barnacle grows right up on top of the poor crab's sex organs and completely destroys them by cutting off nutrients to the tissue.

Next, the barnacle pushes some more of its tendrils up into the brain of the crab and starts monkeying around with the wiring. Firstly, the barnacle shuts off the crab's desire to breed. If you have essentially replaced the vagina of your host with your face, you don't need any crab penises poking you in the eye while you are trying to work.**

With the crab sterilized and permanently unhorny, the barnacle can start the next stage of its seriously messed-up plan.

The pale mass that looks like a cooked scallop located where this poor crab's lady parts should be is the castrator barnacle. A weird, fleshy, brain-hacking, genital-choking barnacle that is sucking the crab's blood and being awful. Photo: Smithsonian Research Institute

In much the same way that the female castrator barnacle entered the crab as a larva, the permanently larval male castrator barnacle finds a host crab that already has a female barnacle infecting it and swims inside his mate's body through a pore on her face because parasitic barnacles are romantic like that.

Once inside, he fertilizes the female barnacle, and she starts producing hundreds of tiny eggs. At this point, the barnacle will hijack the crab's brain again, pulling wires and messing with hormones, thus causing the crab's maternal instincts to kick in. The crab will now care for the growing lump of barnacle eggs on her belly as if they were his own brood, protecting them and using her paddle-like back legs to fan them with fresh oxygenated water. When the time is right, the barnacle pushes some more brain buttons, and the infected crab finds a rock high up in the current and gently brushes the eggs off into the water column to help spread the next generation of life-sucking, gonad-eating parasite's offspring. The only possible problem for the barnacle is that half of the time it infects a male green crab instead of a female.

The reason this is a problem is that male crabs have no maternal instincts to hijack, so the barnacle won't get a free nanny bult into their house/meal. The barnacle has a simple solution to this. It simply starts hacking into the male crab's brain and convinces him to turn into a female. That's right, the castrator barnacle offers free, mandatory, and extremely invasive sex change therapy by getting the crab to start pumping out estrogen like a mare in heat. Once the male crab has been forcibly introduced to his feminine side, he will start acting just like a female crab would. He starts fanning the barnacle's eggs and helps them hatch when the time is right.

So, the next time you are swallowing a penicillin tablet the size of a gumball to get rid of that post-Mardi gras rash, just be glad your venereal disease came with an orgasm instead of a mind-controlling, genital crushing crustacean.

*I never really thought about this but the fact that crab's claws cannot reach their naughty bits means crabs cannot physically masturbate. Just when you thought living in the ocean couldn't suck any more.

**crabs don't have penises and barnacles don't have eyes.

You Could Wait Your Entire Life For Spring Break And Then Die

Waiting for things sucks. Patience is a virtue, and basically all a virtue is, is waiting until you die before you do anything fun in the hopes that there is a paradise waiting for you. That sucks ass. What is the longest time you have waited for something? Whatever the number is, I'll bet you didn't wait seventeen years for it. The same cannot be said for the periodical **cicada**.

Periodical cicadas spend that exact amount of time waiting, in the dark, underground, sucking on a tree root for sustenance. They aren't waiting for anything cool like the next PlayStation console or a solar eclipse or for their dads to come back from the store with that "milk" they needed. They are waiting to be born… sort of. Cicadas are insects that go through incomplete metamorphosis. This means that they go through stages of radical body transformations in order to mature and fall into new niches. Kind of like when the annoyingly vocal abstinence girl goes to college and suddenly becomes promiscuous or whatever happens to goth kids when they grow up.

An adult male 17 year cicada Magicicada septendecula not being nearly active enough considering he only has a few hours left to live. Photo: C. Simon

For a cicada, this metamorphosis is basically a sudden and violent onset of puberty, but instead of growing pubes they grow a bunch of new organs like wings and genitals on the inside and then crack open their skin/bones in order to reveal them. Before that can happen, though, the cicada must do an awful lot of growing. That's where the waiting comes in.

Cicadas start life as an egg abandoned by their parents on some random fucking tree branch. (Are you "abandoned" if your parents die or are you just an orphan?) Once the cicadas hatch, they fall to the ground and burrow into it. At this stage they are called nymphs. The newly buried nymph latches onto a tree root and waits. For seventeen goddamn years. Just sitting in a hole in the ground, sucking on a root in total darkness, alone for seventeen incredibly boring years. That is enough time for a human to go from an infant to someone you can legally have sex with in seven US states. (Twenty if you count ones where sixteen is the age of consent.) That is enough time to be mildly amused by the entire run of the sitcom *Friends,* with time leftover to rewatch the first 7 seasons and be thoroughly unamused right up to Chandler and Monica's wedding in the season finale. That is enough time to walk off 2,980,440 spontaneous erections (WebMD says they last three minutes on average).

Anyway, after waiting the amount of time it takes Mt. Everest to grow 2 ¾ of an inch, periodical cicadas emerge all at once with as many as 1.5 million cicadas per acre. Naturally the first thing on their mind is using their new body parts. Namely, their wings, and more importantly, their 'nads. Does all that patience pay off in the form of a long adult life full of flying and boning? No. Periodical cicadas have about four weeks to live it up before dying down. They spend an incredibly cruel and brief time frantically searching for a mate and hopefully reproducing before plotzing a month later.

A cicada nymph in its burrow, counting out "one-Mississippi, two-Mississippi and so on until seventeen years have passed. I don't care how bad puberty was for you, it is not as bad as sitting in a permanent crunch position with sand on your eyeballs.
Photo: Graham Wise

Now scientists posit that the deafening calls of male cicadas (which can reach an impressive one hundred decibels) are a way of attracting a mate, but that's bullshit. Forget sound amplifying membranes and hollow chambers under the wings. The cicadas are shrieking like that because they just found out they spent seventeen years as an infant so they could live for four measly weeks as an adult. Do you understand that math? These bugs spend 99.996 percent of their lives as a baby, sucking beet juice out of the ground in total darkness, and .004 percent of their lives with functioning genitals. That blows.

You Could Get Your Ass Eaten While On Shrooms And Meth But Like... Not In A Good Way

Remember when I said that periodical cicadas wait seventeen years to emerge from the ground? Well, they aren't the only thing waiting in the soil. Sometimes, when a cicada nymph tunnels down into the soil of the tree it was born under, it comes across a particular fungus known as *Massospora cicadina*.

This fungus settles in next to the nymph, waiting to infect it once the cicada is old enough. Kind of like creeps watching the Olsen twins in the early 2000's. (Gen Z, if you are out there you can substitute Bhad Bhabie in there for that joke and it tracks.)

Once the cicada emerges, *M. cicadina* starts its sickening invasion. The fungus spreads inside the host cicada's abdomen, feeding off the cicada's tissue and tapping into its systems. The fungus starts to produce spores, which form a plug of white, chalky mass that erupts from the cicada's butt and causes the abdomen to fall off. This super fucked-up de-assening does not kill the cicada because the spores seal off the wound and prevent the cicada from bleeding out. The de-assening does, however, make the cicada infertile, which is a dick move. The fungus needs its host to not know that it has been sterilized, but we'll get to that in a moment. Scientists aren't sure how the *Massospora* goes about changing the cicada's behavior, but somehow infected cicadas start acting in the best interest not of themselves, but of the fungus that is eating it from the inside out. Infected cicadas stop flying and drag their infected abdomens over the ground, spreading spores all over the place like a toddler spreading goldfish cracker crumbs over couch cushions.

The Massospora wants to spread, so it makes sure to help its host get laid. Affected by certain compounds that the fungus secretes, infected males sing more aggressively and sometimes imitate the female cicadas mating behavior by sensually flicking its wings. This causes a lot of awkward interactions between the infected males and the confused suitors who try to hump them. "Hey, bro, I'm not a chick, I just can't help moving like one because I have a mushroom growing in my brain. Also, you are a bug zombie now too."

Infected females also act like females except a lot sluttier, being seemingly receptive to any male suitors who will, unbeknownst to them, be trying to impregnate a murderous ball of fungal spores. While scientists do not know how the fungus is able to control the cicada, they have isolated two surprising substances in the bodies of *Massospora*-infected cicadas. Those compounds are psilocybin and amphetamine. That's right; those poor castrated cicadas are being slurped up from the inside out while tripping balls and running on speed. In fairness, if half your body gets eaten by a mushroom, you might need a little pick me up too. To this end, the amphetamine might help the cicadas keep up the energy to keep spreading fungal spores by humping everything while they are being eaten alive. What purpose the psilocybin serves in the mind control process is not understood. My hope is that the *Massospora* produces it as a way of apologizing for forcing its host to use the amputated stump of its ass as a day care for the *Massospora's* babies. "Sorry for killing you in the slowest and most fucked-up way possible. Here's some drugs. Enjoy smelling sounds while I liquify your balls." In my heart I know that's not the case, though. Nature is a whore and the only reason she does anything is so that she can bend you over a coffee table and have her way with you.

Note the advanced stage of decay on this clearly dead infected... ...oh shit, no actually that poor bastard is still alive. The abdomen of this cicada has been almost completely consumed by M. cicadina fungus. The cicada would probably be scream-ing right now if it could, if not for two things; 1) It is tripping its balls off, 2) It doesn't have a voice box. Photo: TelosCricket

For the approximately 5 percent of periodical cicadas who will become infected with *Massospora*, life is somehow even more cruel than it is to the 95 percent who aren't. Not only do they have to spend seven-teen years as a baby, sucking sap out of a mud-covered root so they can spend a month above ground, hopefully screwing and then dying. Infected cicadas have their genitals destroyed, their internal organs slowly digested, their brains taken over, and their reality warped by awesome and/or awful drugs. They will never be able to pass on their genes; they are so lost in the sauce that they spend most of their adulthood humping tree branches or other dudes, and the always lethal infection kills them even faster than their own design would.

You Could Have Your Tongue Cut Out And Replaced With A Giant Bug-Crab-Thing

In keeping with the theme of parasites replacing parts of their hosts' body in disgusting ways (by this point in the book you should know not to be eating while reading), you could be a fish with an **isopod** instead of a tongue. If you aren't familiar with isopods, don't worry. You have actually seen a member of this order before. The wood louse is a general name for a widespread group of isopod species that you may have grown up calling a **pill bug**, roly-poly, or sow bug in America and a bunch of cheese or pig related things everywhere else in the world. Anyway, these cute little armored crustaceans that look like someone cut out the middle of a millipede evolved from marine isopods who crawled out of the water somewhere in the carboniferous period.

These isopods -some of whom can get disturbingly large- usually live in the deep sea where the only thing they can terrify are equally scary looking. However, like most groups of animals, some isopod species eventually figured out that they could have a much easier time feeding off someone else's hard work/body and went the parasitic route. Some species live on the skin of their fish hosts, some live on the gills of shrimp, and the list goes on. While all forms of **parasitism** are unequivocally a **dick move**, one genus of isopod takes the cake for taking the tongue of its host.

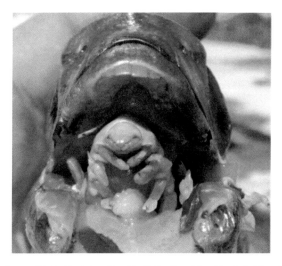

Above: Holy Fucking Shit Balls! What The Fuck Is That?!

Cymothoa exigua is a species of marine isopod also called the tongue-eating louse. The tongue-eating louse swims into the gills of a host fish and makes itself at home. If it is a male louse, it will stay here, feeding on the blood and mucus produced by the host. If it is a female tongue-eating louse, it will move through the gills and up to the mouth. Using her pincerlike front legs, the tongue-eating louse will sever the blood vessels leading to the tongue, causing the tissue to die. The tongue-eating louse then eats the tongue (bet you never saw that coming) and uses its other legs to attach itself to the cartilaginous base of the former tongue.

In this way the tongue-eating louse essentially becomes the tongue of the fish, staying there for the rest of the fish's life. I should mention that it seemed in my research that scientists were going out of the way to point out that the louse doesn't seem to inhibit the function of the fish, and besides cutting the fish's tongue off, the louse doesn't do any further damage to the fish. I'm not sure who they interviewed for that research paper, but I'll bet it wasn't the fish who just got its goddamn tongue cut off by an underwater centipede.

"Yeah, no, I mean sure he barged into my mouth by pushing my extremely fragile and sensitive gills out of the way and cut my fucking tongue out and ate it while still inside of me, but yeah, he didn't really hurt anybody in the long run. I mean sure he will be stealing my blood and eating my food before I can swallow it but at least I am never, ever going to be able to kiss anyone ever again." – said every fish with a tongue-eating louse.

You Could Have Your Eyeballs Hijacked By A Suicidal Worm

Imagine that you are walking along a bridge, and you see a person about to jump to their death. You're a good person, right? (Honestly if you have made it this far in the book and are still enjoying yourself that may not be true.) For the sake of this analogy, we will say you would try to intervene. You cautiously approach and urge the person to rethink their decision. You talk to him, try to empathize and try to make a connection with him. Things get emotional but eventually he takes a step back from the ledge. He starts to cry. You embrace him and say, "It won't always be this way. Things will get better, I promise."

The man wipes the tears from his eyes and says, "Thank you, I couldn't do this without you." He reaches out with his hand, and you shake it firmly, saying, "You're welcome. Now go live your life."

He smiles and says, "No." He then grabs you by the collar and leaps backward, pulling you both to your death on the rocks below.

What the fuck, right? You want to kill yourself that's your prerogative, but don't take somebody else with you. That is some bitch-ass school shooter shit. And yet, making a non-optional suicide pact with a stranger is not exclusive to imaginary bridge jumpers or deranged youths. There is a particularly dickish worm that yearns for the void and insists on bringing a friend along for the ride.

The tangle of roots with zombie tampons growing out of it is actually the mature sporocyst of the parasitic flatworm: Leucochloridium paradoxum.

Meet **Leucochloridium paradoxum.** This parasitic flatworm infects the rectums of a variety of passerine birds such as crows, blue jays, and sparrows. How it gets there is by way of an unwitting amber snail. Before we get into that, though, it is worth talking for a moment about snails in general.

Evolution is the gift that keeps on screwing (literally and metaphorically), and snails got the Darwinian shaft in a number of ways. They have eyes that look like they should be fairly useful, but they suck. Think Velma without her glasses at night. Snail eyes can basically just sense light and dark. In addition to that, they have no arms and only one foot. Actually, it's worse than that. They don't just *have* one foot they *are* a foot.

Actually, it is a bit more complicated than just being a foot. Hold on, I should have just done this before...

You Could Be A Goddamn Snail

Now where were we? Ah yes, snails are a foot with shitty eyes and a shell. Well, yes, but there's more.

Imagine that you were flexible enough to touch your chin to the top of your feet while standing. Now hold that position. You are basically folded in half. Now imagine that every limb that is touching fuses together. That is, your legs and arm become one, your neck fuses to your ankles and your head becomes the top of your feet-foot. Go ahead and nix all of the bones and limbs because snails have neither.

If you pictured that properly, you should be seeing a giant foot with an amorphous blob of organs and flesh perched on its back, with a butthole at the top of it. The front of the foot has a head sticking out of it. Now slap a shell on all that back stuff and call it a day. Right after you figure out where to put all the holes.

The ear holes? Don't need 'em because you don't have ears. Nostrils? Turn them inside out and double them. Your nose just became two sets of tentacles that can smell. The upper set also happens to be your eyes. (This explains why snails suck so bad at seeing, they are looking out the end of an inverted sneezer.) The mouth gets pushed through the foot and out the bottom so that is pretty straightforward. (speaking of mouths, your teeth will migrate to your tongue where they will make a sort of rake called a ragellum. In practice, this means that you eat by scraping your prickly tongue against the ground and licking up whatever gets sloughed off.) The genitals need to come out somewhere and don't forget snails are **hermaphrodites** so you got an inney and an outey that must be considered. You can't tuck them in the shell, or it might be hard to mate, so put the opening in the bottom of the foot about two-thirds of the way up where you think an armpit should be. The last hole you need to worry about is the anus, that can also not stay where it is, or it will be shoved way into the back of that stupid shell. Having your ass empty out into your shell would basically turn it into a diaper you can never change. So, move it to the only logical place left which is of course, the top of your head.

I'm sure there is some good reason why the anus couldn't empty out onto the bottom of the foot or the tail end of it, but I'm just saying, I would much rather have shit on the bottom of my foot than running down the back of my neck.

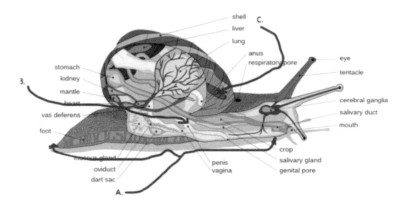

A detailed illustration of snail anatomy. Notice the theme of multi-use body parts.
Foot/body
Combination penis and vagina (if you impregnate yourself is it still incest?)
Butthole/neck

On top of their rather unfortunate anatomy, the snail is relegated to inching along at glacial speeds, helped along by a disgusting mucus lubricant that it must constantly lay down. It is like having a runny nose except your whole body is "runny" and you are lying in it. The snail crawls along, munching on whatever plant material it comes across and pooping on its head. Speaking of poop, the snail has a habit of ingesting it on a somewhat regular basis. Due to the aforementioned terrible eyesight, the snail has a hard time eating around the parts of the leaves it eats that have been shit on. Some of that poop comes from birds and some of that bird poop is hiding eggs in it. Which brings us back to *Leucochloridium paradoxum*.

You Could Have Your Eyeballs Hijacked By A Suicidal Worm Part II

Okay, so a vision-impaired amber snail slurps up some bird shit with a few dozen *Leucochloridium* eggs in it. The eggs travel through the snail's GI tract and set up shop in the snail's liver. From there, it hatches and starts sending out little tendrils throughout the snail's body, siphoning off nutrients directly from the snail's tissue. The *Leucochloridium* uses all this stolen energy to produce at least one, but sometimes several spore bodies. These are the most worm-looking parts of the *Leucochloridium*. They are plump white and green banded tubes that grow out of thin stalks that connect it to the rootlike body of the worm.

The amber snail (Succinea putris) on the left is a healthy gastropod, sliming its way through life. The amber snail on the right has a parasitic flatworm sucking nutrients out of its organs, controlling its brain and pushing a disgusting brood sac into its eye.

These spore bodies push forward through the snail's tissues until they reach its eyes. Somewhere in your childhood you probably poked a snail (or slug; they are basically naked snails) in the eye and saw it retract the long stalk it is extended from. For some reason science dweebs call these appendages "tentacles" which is really stupid because everybody knows what a tentacle is. Tentacles belong on things like squids and octopuses and niche anime porn, and they sure as shit don't have eyes on the end of them. Well, maybe the porn ones do- I don't know, not my cup of tea. Regardless, the spore bodies push their brightly colored bodies into the snail's tentacle. All that extra meat in there causes the tentacle to become permanently extended. Once situated, the *Leucochloridium* spore body starts dancing its creepy little ass off. It pulsates and engorges itself, flashing those bright stripes in hopes of attracting attention to the snail. The spore is trying to look like a tasty caterpillar so that a hungry bird will come and peck the snail's eyes out. Super messed up, right?

As previously stated, the spore's sadomasochistic obsession with being eaten is driven by its need to end up in the GI tract of a bird so that it can grow and lay eggs. In order for the spore to get there, though, it has to be seen. All that dancing and gyrating won't help if the snail stays in the dark. To this end, the *Leucochloridium* has another trick up its sleeve. Somehow, the *Leucochloridium* is able to hijack the part of the snail's brain that tells it to stay in the shade. Infected snails will waltz right out in the open and hang out in the sun waiting for a bird to rip its face off. Scientists think it accomplishes this by employing witchcraft. Well, technically they use the term "chemistry", but it is the same thing.

So, the poor snail wanders out onto an exposed leaf, and his eyeballs start doing the electric slide. A bird takes notice, flies down, rips the eye-stalk out, and leaves the mutilated snail to bake in the sun. This isn't curtains for the unfortunate gastropod, though. The snail can grow those eyes back and if he is lucky, he can live a somewhat normal life. I say somewhat because we are unaware of the existence of snail therapy and the affected individuals could really use some. If the snail is unlucky the bird will rip off a little too much meat and decapitate the little bastard, and he will die. If he is very unlucky, he will heal, go about his snail day, come across another piece of spore infected bird doo-doo and get reinfected by another *Leucochloridium* spore all over again.

Probably the most messed up part of this is that if a *Leucochloridium* spore dances a little too enthusiastically it can rupture the eyestalk of the snail host and flop out onto the ground. If this happens then the *Leucochloridium* spore… is fine! It just keeps dancing. Turns out it doesn't really need the snail for that part. It can lure in a bird and still fulfill its suicidal wish and nobody's eye would have to be pecked out to accomplish it. The worm could have evolved to burst out of the snail's side and pinch itself off and nobody would be forced to have their eyeballs invaded and then violently removed. That would be too easy though. So, the worms continue to infect the poor snails and lure them to their mutilation through no fault of the snail's. In fact, its only crime is that the snail's stupid nose-eyes aren't good at picking out poopy leaves vs. non-poopy leaves. There is a cruel irony inferred from the fact that it is the snail's poor eyesight that leads to its eyes being ripped out of its head in the first place.

I'm not sure what amber snails did to the almighty to earn such a raw deal, but they really must have pissed somebody off. The next time you eat out at the Dutch Country Inn and get a stomach bug, be glad that the side effects are bubble butt and vomiting and not a flesh-eating parasite that migrates from your liver to your eyeballs and takes over your brain.

You Could Have (Barely) Survived Thirty Out of Thirty-One Attempts To Murder You

The year is 1933 and you are a raging alcoholic living during **prohibition**. The lack of legal drinking venues means that you must visit some pretty seedy establishments to wet your whistle. The fact that you are unemployed makes getting credit at these establishments even harder. This is the predicament that one **Michael Malloy** found himself in.

The last watering hole that would still honor Malloy's tab was called "Marino's". It was a **speakeasy** hidden behind an abandoned storefront in a shady corner of Depression-era New York City (which I realize is a redundant statement). Unbeknownst to Malloy, his new drinking buddies had decided that he would be a good candidate for an insurance fraud claim. The bar's regulars had listened to Malloy's slurred rantings for long enough to know that he had no friends or family to come sniffing around, and his general lack of hygiene and the fact that the only thing anyone had ever seen him eat was whiskey gave the conspirators reason to believe that poor Michael Malloy was not long for this world.

The owner of the bar was a charming, god-fearing man named Tony Marino who had previously scammed a life insurance company by collecting the payout after his girlfriend tragically died. The girlfriend in question died from **pneumonia** after passing out drunk next to an open window in the winter. A window that just happened to be opened by Tony after he'd stripped her naked and poured water over her. You know, the same way you tuck your girlfriend into bed after one too many Whiteclaws.

A still "heart-broken" Tony figured that it would be a shame if another destitute drunk were to die without anyone benefitting from their death, and so he and a few of the other scumbags at Marino's hatched a simple but elegant plan to kill Michael Malloy. The plan was simply to give Malloy a limitless bar tab and let his alcoholism take care of the rest. Through various unscrupulous means, the group took out three separate policies on Malloy using fake names and managed to get the bartender of Marino's penned as the sole heir.

The first night of the plot went off easily enough. Malloy was informed of his new credit and proceeded to drink himself silly. The group watched from their stools as he got completely shitfaced and stumbled out of the bar alive. For three more nights Malloy would walk in, drink enough liquor to drown a sailor, and yodel his way out to the street and into the night. After several days of this, the group was getting impatient and decided that they should speed things along a little. One of the party suggested mixing **wood alcohol** in with Malloy's shots, and the others agreed. Wood alcohol or methanol is often used in anti-freeze and paint thinners and when ingested even in very small amounts can cause blindness and death. After Malloy was sufficiently lubed up on regular booze, the conspirators mixed the wood alcohol in with his shots and crossed their fingers. Malloy knocked back shot after shot with his usual enthusiasm with no negative side effects. That is to say, no fatal side effects. Repeatedly pissing down your leg and being such an obnoxious, useless boozer that people openly plan to kill you, and nobody talks them out of it is definitely a negative side effect of severe alcoholism.

Over the next couple of days, the "Murder Trust", as they were eventually called, gradually upped the ratio of wood alcohol to whiskey in Malloy's drinks… with no luck. Eventually they switched to just straight wood alcohol, and all they succeeded in doing was getting Malloy to finally pass out in the bar instead of outside of it. The next day someone suggested that they soak some oysters in wood alcohol and give them to Malloy, who ate as many as they had prepared without dying. Next, the group left sardines out to rot for a few days and made a sandwich with the fish and a few carpet tacks (some sources say glass or metal shavings) and gave it to Malloy. I do not know how fucked up you must be to not notice nails or glass in your food, but apparently Malloy not only did not notice but asked for another sandwich.

Poisoning Malloy was starting to cost a lot of money. Weeks of free drinks to a champion boozer and now the cost of tainted meals was adding up. Put that on top of the monthly insurance payments, and it was starting to look like the Murder Trust was going to lose money on this deal. Tony "#1 boyfriend" Marino decided to go back to his roots and suggested freezing Malloy instead of poisoning him.

After Malloy's nightly binge nap had started, some of the Murder Trust brought him to a park bench and poured gallons of water over the shirtless Malloy. Convinced that the man would soon succumb to the New York winter, the men went home. The next day, when the group got to Marino's, a sniffly and thirsty Malloy was already waiting for them. One of the frustrated plotters had to be talked out of shooting Malloy in the head right there and then, and instead they decided to try helping Malloy find his way into a car accident.

The now very impatient Murder Trust waited until Malloy passed out, took him to the street, and held him up as another conspirator attempted to run Malloy down with his taxi. Malloy somehow managed to stumble out of the way twice before being more thoroughly propped up by his would-be killers. The third attempt succeeded, and Malloy was thrown up and over the car and onto the ground behind it. The driver backed up over his body to ensure that the unbelievably resilient wino was actually dead. The members of the Trust fled the scene and waited for word.

The next day was the first time in months that old Michael Malloy hadn't dragged himself into Marino's speakeasy, and the Murder Trust was starting to smile. The only problem was that nobody was reporting a fatal hit and run. Without the body, they didn't have anything with which to claim the insurance payout. The Murder Trust actually went out and hit some other poor bastard with their car, but he lived and fucked off and out of the story after that. Five days later, the now very battered but somehow still breathing Malloy explained that he had woken up in a hospital with a fractured skull, broken bones in his arm and shoulder. He had no memory of what happened, and he said he really just needed a drink. The dumbfounded and very annoyed murder trust obliged Malloy yet again and decided that once he had drunken himself into his usual stupor, they would finally finish the job and make sure of it this time.

After renting a room for Malloy under a fake name, the group dragged the bruised and broken Malloy into a cramped room and hooked his face up to a furnace exhaust with some tape, a hose and some towels to seal it off. At long last nobody was trying to kill Michael Malloy anymore... because he was dead. Tony Marino and his co-conspirators were quickly discovered when the insurance company ordered an autopsy, and they were all found guilty of murder and about a million attempted murders.

The next time you are nursing a hangover just be glad that your drinks weren't made with anti-freeze, your beer munchies did not lead you to consume poisoned oysters and your friends aren't actively and repeatedly trying to kill you.

You Could Have Had The Bloodiest War In American History Start And End In Your House

Wilmer McLean was a good old Virginia boy who lived near Manassas, Virginia, in 1861. The **American Civil War** had just broken out, and the Northern and Southern armies were about to come to blows in the first major battle of the war. A key railroad junction near Manassas was targeted by both sides, and McLean's farm was determined to be good shootin' ground.

The terrain was favorable for the absurd style of combat still being practiced in those days. Namely: marching stoically forward while taking turns shooting variously sized lead balls at one another to the sound of flute music. Being a Southern man, McLean enthusiastically offered his house up as the Confederate headquarters for the duration of the battle. For his trouble, he returned to find dead people all over the yard and several cannon holes through his kitchen.

The Confederates won the battle, which, depending on which side you were on, was called either The First Battle of Bull Run or The First Battle of Manassas. However (spoiler alert), the fight for Manassas Junction was not over, as evidenced by the creatively named "Second Battle of Bull Run/Manassas," which took place a little over a year later at- you guessed it- Manassas Junction. This even bloodier battle resulted in another Confederate victory.

Wilmer McLean (pictured above) with a "I'm pretty sick of this war shit happening on my lawn" expression on his face. Photo: National Park Service

Wilmer McLean was not there to watch the second battle of whatever-the-hell-you-want-to-call-it and the carnage it brought to his farmhouse because he had moved about a hundred miles south to get away from the war. McLean spent the next several years working as a supply partner for the Confederate Army and then as a sugar speculator operating out of his home in Appomattox Court House. I should clarify that he did not live in a courthouse; the name of the town was Appomattox Court House. Apparently in the more bumble-fuck rural areas of Virginia it was common to name county seats by adding "court house" to the end of their name.

Now that we have that out of the way, if you weren't stoned or asleep through history class you may remember that the po-dunk little town of

Appomattox Court House has some significance in the Civil War. Namely, it ended there.

When General Robert E. Lee realized that he was cut off from reinforcements, the Confederate capital of Richmond had been captured, and his starving and exhausted troops were officially boned, he asked his staff to find a suitable place to formally surrender.

Apparently the first citizen of Appomattox that they ran into was the very same Wilmer McLean who had volunteered his property for use at the beginning of the war. McLean somewhat reluctantly offered up his new home after remembering what had happened the last time he'd let Johnny Reb' stay the night, and the stage was set. Later that day, General Robert E. Lee offered his surrender to Union General Ulysses S. Grant with the only condition being that every other high school south of the Mason-Dixon line be named after him.

So, the war ended, and everybody was happy! Well, everyone except for all the starving, defeated, suddenly unemployed confederate soldiers, and Mr. Wilmer McLean. You would think McLean would be happy being the owner of two future historic landmarks, but he couldn't really think about that because everyone who had been present at the signing had ransacked his house of anything remotely connected to the momentous occasion. The troops made off with his furniture, cut fabric from his upholstery and absconded with anything that wasn't tied down. One weirdo had even made off with McLean's seven-year-old daughter's ragdoll. Wilmer McLean watched his first home get destroyed by cannonballs, his crops trampled, his fields filled with corpses and craters and his barn stained with the blood of dozens of "surgeries" at the start of the war. His second property was smack dab in the middle of another battle, his land used to house weary soldiers and his home was pillaged for war memorabilia.

Wilmer McLean was pretty sick of being in the middle of historical events and rightfully so. He would default on his mortgage payments at the house where Lee surrendered, probably because he had to spend all his bill-paying money buying new shit to sit on and sleep under. McLean would take his family back to Manassas to live in the shit-hole house with the cannon ball holes in the kitchen and would work for the IRS until 1876, dying 6 years later.

Jesus, that is a depressing sentence. If you ever get pissed to find a jury summons in your mailbox take comfort in knowing that your government could have asked you to host a war at your house.

You Could Go Down In History As The Man To Do More Environmental Harm to Planet Earth Than Any Other Human Ever

That's crazy right because fucking up the planet is kind of our thing as people. Despite lots and lots of trying by many people over a long and storied history of pollution, only one man stands atop the steaming landfill that is human civilization's poisonous history.

That man is **Thomas Midgley Jr.** In 1921, Midgley was working on the problem of **engine knock** at his job as an engineer at the Dayton Research Laboratories of General Motors. Engine knock is a problematic condition inside combustion engines whereby fuel ignites prematurely and detonates which causes excess pressure in the cylinder and often times damages the engine. This damage can be minor such as dimpling or pitting of cylinder walls, or it can be catastrophic like when the engine of my 1994 Geo Tracker exploded on the highway a month after I bought it. I didn't DO anything to it Randy. It was a piece of shit when you sold it to me, you weasel!

Thomas Midgley Jr. American chemist and engineer. Most famous for inventing anti-knock leaded gasoline and synthesizing the first CFC refrigerant. Dude was basically the Tony Stark of fucking up the planet.

Anyways, Midgley discovered that by adding small amounts of **tetraethyl lead** to gasoline he could virtually eliminate engine knocking. The discovery was a game changer, and the market for Midgley's fuel additive soared. The only problem was that working with lead, let alone burning it with gasoline in your car, is not very healthy. Between 1923 and 1924, fifteen people would die at factories associated with the production of tetraethyl lead (TEL), and dozens more would become seriously ill. People were dropping left and right, and nobody knew why. Just kidding; it was the fucking lead and pretty much everybody at General Motors and DuPont knew it! The dangers of handling lead had been known for generations. In fact, Benjamin Franklin had written about the health risks of lead 137 years earlier. Midgley and his team of profit hungry eggheads claimed that the levels of lead being released into the air would have little health effects which is weird because the same year that he filed his patent for TEL, Midgley would be treated for goddamn lead poisoning! The subsequent years saw virtually the entire mechanized world adopt leaded gasoline as the primary fuel for their engines and not surprisingly, the levels of lead in the atmosphere sky-rocketed.

Exposure to lead has many adverse effects and can lead to high blood pressure, joint pain, birth defects, aggression, seizures, organ failure and even death. In fact, the correlation between aggression and lead poisoning is so strong that a side by side graph of homicide rates and atmospheric lead in the United States tracks almost identically. In 1971, the United States finally got around to phasing out leaded gasoline after a sufficient number of people went psycho and died very twitchy deaths after shooting night clerks at 7-11s. The process of moving away from TEL would continue globally and would not actually conclude until -holy shit- 2021! The last country to deplete its stocks of leaded gasoline was Algeria, doing so nearly one hundred years after it was invented.

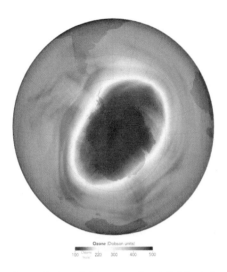

The hole in the ozone layer depicted 76 years after Midgley's death, as it was on Oct. 5th 2022 when it reached its largest size in area for that year. If there is ever any doubt, you know you made a pretty big oopsie if it can be seen from space. NASA Photo: Joshua Stevens

Back in the 1920's, Midgley was working on another chemical problem. Or should I say, making one. Refrigerants of the time were either highly flammable or highly toxic, which is sort of funny thing to worry about coming from the people that just patented lead aerosols, but whatever. Midgley's mastery of chemistry culminated in him synthesizing the first Chlorofluorocarbon (CFC). He patented his invention as R-12 under the commercial name "Freon". This new refrigerant was non-flammable and less toxic (to people) than any previous compounds. This made it ideal for commercial use, and it would become extremely popular. Unlike lead, CFC's environmental impact would not be known for several decades. The harmful chemicals would be used in everything from minifridges to aerosols and even freaking asthma inhalers before being outlawed in 1989. While they were being used though, CFC's were quietly burning a hole through the Earth's ozone layer, cooking the South Pole and contributing extensively to global warming.

While Thomas Midgley's inventions were quietly poisoning the kids and decimating the atmosphere, the effects they had on industry were earning him awards left and right. He was given several honors from various nerdy societies, elected to the US National Academy of the Sciences and made president of The American Chemical Society. In 1941 Midgley contracted polio, and his health quickly deteriorated. Like everything Midgley made, his final invention was disastrous, but this time it was deadly only to himself. Midgley had constructed an elaborate pulley system to allow him to get in and out of bed on his own. While it was a clever bit of engineering, in 1944 he was found dead by way of strangulation, entangled in the ropes of his contraption.

Midgley's legacy is one of environmental catastrophe. His inventions caused lifelong health problems and death all around the globe. Humans and indeed every living thing have been touched by the effects of his creations. I like to think of old Tom standing next to his marionette-like corpse and asking the grim reaper if he made a difference in the world and the reaper tries to hold back laughter and just says, "Yeeeeeah, you could say that."

Midgley's story is often told as one of genius and unintended consequences; the tragic outcome of the best of intentions. Fuck that. Midgley got lead poisoning from his own "perfectly safe" invention, oversaw the factory where dozens of his employees were going screwy and straight up dying and did nothing. He actively suppressed the effects of TEL from the public and I don't care what they say they knew about CFC's there is no fucking way you can be a chemist and think putting chlorine and fluorine together in a kid's inhaler is going to be okay for anyone. Despite his intentions, Midgley became the closest thing the planet has seen to a real super villain; churning out low key doomsday weapons like they were Marvel movies and slowly poisoning the entire planet. The next time you accidentally make things worse when you are trying to help, remember that you couldn't possibly have a worse outcome than the man who dissolved the ozone layer and gave 80 percent of the world lead poisoning before he was middle-aged.

You Could Be The Author Of This Book Compiling The Most Fucked Up And Depressing Stories He Could Find, Consuming All Of It & Putting It Together Here With Like A 2% Chance Of Actually Profiting Off The Damn Thing

Do you have any idea how many different ways there are to die in a shipwreck? Or how many people wrote detailed diaries of watching helpless innocent travelers die in agonizing ways? Do you know how many videos of hyenas ripping the testicles off of African game I had to watch before I found an image I could use without licensing problems? Do you have any idea how much a zebra's penis can stretch before it tears to the sound of agony and blood spurting out of arteries?

I researched people dying, getting maimed, electrocuted, struck by celestial objects. I spent three whole months watching parasitic worms wriggle around in various creatures for research. My search history is so strange that I got a call from the NSA asking me to tone it down for the sake of their surveillance computer. I said, "Computer? It isn't a person?" They told me that they usually are, but mine killed himself after six months of screening my internet time. Once the computer started disassociating from his work colleagues and was having trouble at home, they knew they had to step in.

I have seen dolphins raping people. People raping dolphins. I scrolled through the darkest subreddits you can find and got cyber-bullied by preteen internet trolls. I saw things I will never unsee and I did all of that while ignoring the cries and whimpers from my infant son. Well, he was an infant. Now he is two years old and I missed all of it because my nose was buried in the blackest pages of human history all for a passion project that is almost certainly not going to pay for my son's college. I have zero movie credits, not nearly enough Instagram followers, and no intriguing affairs with current or former presidents to prop up this book. That is a long way of saying that I will sell probably three copies of this thing and one of them is going to be to my mom who will absolutely hate it because of all the fucking swearing. My only hope that somehow, a twisted and tortured mind such as yours meets all the algorithmic requirements to see this tome appear in your "suggested for you" ticker on Amazon and my works gives you the strength to carry through another day. I hope you laughed and learned something. Preferably something that will bewilder and horrify party guests when you bring it up in casual conversation. Thank you for reading, and remember: It could be worse.

Epilogue

Well that was a lot huh? We learned about testicle-munching mollusks, testicle-munching hyenas and testicle-munching fungus. We learned that the safest place to be post-gunshot wound, in the time before germ theory, is as far away from a doctor as you can manage. We also learned that there are not nearly enough barriers to keep just anyone from writing a book.

When I first started this project I thought I knew what I wanted it to be. I wanted it to be stupid in the smartest way possible. I imagined my readers on the toilet or ignoring their studies or wrapping this up as a white elephant present to be discarded on a hapless in-law or coworker. What I didn't realize is that it would go on to become a massive, multi-million dollar best-seller that has become the very pinnacle of wit and humor, bringing me wealth and fame far beyond my wildest dreams. To be clear, that has not happened yet and probably won't. In fact, I will be shocked if I don't lose money on this little endeavor. For what it's worth, I tried making a sex tape to get some free press but that apparently only works in specific circumstances. No matter, I will keep my schedule open in case any late night shows come calling. If I claimed this book got me pregnant do you think I could be on Paternity Court? I digress…

In all seriousness, I thought the only person that would benfit from this book would be me. I would realize my childhood dream of becoming a writer and I could finally go to bed without hating myself for not finishing the damn thing. What I truly hope is that however many copies actually get sold, you, the reader, get some value in its pages from something that has helped me through my struggles with mental health. I have tried therapy, drugs, lame drugs that I was actually prescribed, and various other remedies for despair. The thing that has given me the greatest relief has always been laughter. Seeing the humor in this crazy, messed up world and sharing it with others. Like hallucinogen-laced popcorn, the effects of laughter do eventually wear off but if you know where to look, it is not that hard to find. Some people find it in cat videos and some people find it in irreverant descriptions of horrific boating accidents. This world is too interesting and too damn funny to leave. If you are struggling in the ways I have struggled, I hope that you think so too and I hope something in this book spurred enough interest or disgust in your mind to convince you to stick around to learn more about it.

Speaking of learning more about it, check out my works cited for links to all of the crazy corners of the web and forgotten tomes that helped inform this book. You will learn so much more than what is collected here and provide you with even more fuel for your comparative suffering portfolio.

Thank you for taking this journey with me and look out for the movie adaptation of this book which will be coming out some time next year. (My friend Ashley who legally changed her middle name to "Moonrise Ayahuasca Soulbloom " calls that manifesting…we'll see Ashley. I'm keeping my fingers crossed for the A.I. ressurrected voice of Gilbert Gottfried to do the narration.) For the rest of you, remember: It could be worse.

Glossary of Terms

A

Abraham Lincoln: The sixteenth President of The United States. Lincoln held office during the Civil War, signed the Emancipation Proclamation that freed all slaves in the United States, and wasn't a big fan of the play "Our American Cousin." President Lincoln is said to have looked remarkably like actor Daniel Day Lewis with a beard, and is enshrined in the WWE Hall of Fame along with another US president, Donald J. Trump. (The last part sounds fake but is actually true. Lincoln was an accomplished greco-roman wrestler and Donnie appeared several times on WWE broadcasts before becoming POTUS.)

Adam and Eve: In Judeo-Christian tradition they were the first two people, hand made by God. The book of Genesis says that they lived 930 years and populated the Earth in that time. That is a lot of incest.

Alabama: The twenty-second state admitted into the United States of America. Home to the University of Alabama college football team, which is really good, and lots of historic racism, which is bad. Alabama is notably not nearly as bad as everyone thinks when it comes to boinking one's relatives, having outlawed the practice In 1975. (New Jersey and Rhode island have zero laws governing sexual contact between consenting adults regardless of familial ties so... ...if that special someone already has your last name before you even started dating, consider Jersey or Rhode Island for the nuptials.)

Alexander Graham Bell: A Scottish-born American inventor, teacher, scientist and engineer who introduced Hellen Keller to her tutor Ann Sullivan, received a middle name as a birthday present when he turned eleven and tried in vain to help find an assassin's bullet in President Garfield's torso.

His company, the Bell Grammaphone Company would eventually become AT&T, so I guess I can blame Bell for those jackals raising my rates every year when I make a new account with a fake email. Oh, and he invented the telephone.

American Civil War: A small disagreement spanning April 12, 1861 – May 26, 1865, involving the Union (northern states) and the Confederacy (southern states) in the US. Honestly, I hesitate to call it a disagreement since it was more of a spat. A tiff, if you will. This little difference of opinion led to the bloodiest conflict in American history with an estimated 1.5 million military casualties and five hundred thousand to one million dead civilians.

Ambulatory: In a medical sense it means you are capable of moving. The word comes from the Latin term for walking: *ambulare*. The French word for walking was ambulant. They called field hospitals "hopital ambulant" meaning mobile hospital or literally walking hospital. They later started to refer to the wagons that brought soldiers to the field hospitals as ambulance wagons which later was simplified to just ambulance which we still use today to refer to a vehicle that transports people to hospitals. It is helpful to remember the root of the word ambulance if you ever find yourself in need of medical transportation because the bill you will receive after using an ambulance will make you wish you had just walked to the hospital instead.

Anglerfish: The common name for fish species of the order *Lophiiformes*. These diverse fish belonging to sixteen separate families are universally carnivourous, and hunt through a variety of methods. Some anglerfish are ambush hunters and others use a visual or olfactory lure that extends from the top of their head in order to trick prey into striking range. It is for this reason that other fish call anglers the "Judas of the Sea".

Annelida: The phylum containing the "segmented worms" such as earthworms and leeches. twenty-two thousand known species. The word "*annelid*" is an amalgamation of the Latin words for "little" and "anuses".

Ann Elizabeth Hodges: Alabama native and winner of the "worst possible place wherein to be asleep when a meteorite crashes through your roof" award. Ann is the only known person to be hit by a space rock.

Anti-Defamation League: A Jewish non-profit specializing in civil rights law that operates internationally. Founded in 1913 in the aftermath of a highly prejudicial murder conviction, the group sussessfully persuaded the Georgia governor to commute the death sentence of the accused to life in prison instead. An angry mob then kidnapped the defendant and murdered him so it wasn't necessarily the best start. Since that time they have become a leading organization in many aspects of civil law and fighting different kinds of discrimination.

Aplastic anemia: A blood disorder that results in a rapid decline in the body's production of blood cells of all types. In humans it is caused most often by cancer, exposure to certain chemicals, or contact with radioactive material. In ferrets it is caused by not getting laid.

Arabian sand boa: dumbest-looking reptile in the known universe.

Argentina: The second-largest country in South America after Brazil and definitely not where Adolf Hitler moved to after faking his death at the end of WWII. Argentina was once an extremely wealthy country. Its GDP per capita was greater than the United States until 1896. The country remained an economic powerhouse until the Great Depression greatly depressed it.

Australia: Not Austria.

Auto-evisceration: An extremely metal defense mechanism practiced by Holothuroideans (sea cucumbers) in which they forcibly expel various organs and connective tissue through their ass to distract and entangle predators. The first sea cucumber to shit out its lungs when it got scared must have been very relieved to find out that it could regrow them.

B

Battle of Ramree Island: A battle fought during WWII on Ramree Island, Burma. The main combatants were soldiers from Britian and Japan, as well as an unknown number of saltwater crocodiles. What the fuck is right.

Boomslang: The common name for *Dispholidus typus;* a species of venomous snake native to Africa. Known for its extremely potent hemotoxic venom and kickass name.

Bioluminescence: A completely fucking bonkers physical adaptation whereby an organism creates and emits visible light from its body. The organism can make actual light, often on demand, by utilizing either symbiotic bacteria in specialized cells or by producing the light itself. A variety of organisms have independently evolved this ability with at least forty different evolution events being identified.

Blistering: An absurd "medical" procedure wherein the patient is intentionally burned by applying direct heat or caustic chemicals to their afflicted body parts. The purpose of this useless practice was to drain the resulting blister in order to rebalance the humors of the body.

Blizzard: A video game publishing company founded in 1991 and subsequently acquired by Activision known for such titles as World of Warcraft, Diablo, Starcraft and Overwatch. Also the name of a kind of snowstorm defined by the American National Weather Service as a severe snowstorm with heavy snow fall, reduced visibility and sustained winds or frequent gusts of 35mph.

Brazilian wandering spider: The common name of spiders belong to the *Phoneutria* genus that live mainly in South America. These spiders are characterized by their large size (5-7 inches), warning stripes running the length of the underside of their legs, and the ability to give involuntary erections to human males who are bitten by them.

Brothers Grimm: Jacob Grimm(1785–1863) and Wilhelm Grimm (1786–1859) were German academics, cultural researchers, and authors who delighted in scaring the ever-living-shit out of children with their collections of traditional German folklore, which they published in several collections.

C

Cannibalism: The practice of eating a member of one's own species. At least fifteen hundred species are known to engage in some form of cannibalism. Some fun forms of cannibalism are as follows: Sexual cannibalism is where the female eats the male during or after mating. Oophagic cannibalism is when a developing embryo eats the eggs of its younger siblings while still in the womb. This is most spectacularly displayed by species of Lamniformes sharks such as the sand tiger shark. Developing sand tiger sharks will hunt their siblings while in utero. Autocannibalism is considered by some extremely dramatic people to include eating one's nails or peeled skin. The sea squirt (*Ascidiacea*) does it for real. When the juvenile sea squirt attaches itself to a rock to begin its sedentary adult lifestyle it eats its own brain. That's a little more serious than nail biting Jen, you attention whore.

Carnivore: An organism that consumes animal tissue. The word is a combination of the Greek words "Car" meaning "automobile" and "nivore" meaning "no suggestion, check for spelling error".

Castrator barnacle: The common name for the *Sacculina carcini* barnacle, a species of mollusk that parasitizes green crabs in a very specific and shitty way.

Cat: The common name for members of the carnivorous mammalian species *Felis catus*. This common house pet has been domesticated since at least 7500 BC and holds the unenviable title of the second most destructive animal on the planet behind humans. The domestic cat has hunted at least sixty-three different species of animals to extinction and threatens hundreds of endangered species all around the world. I mean, they are probably not a threat to gorillas or tigers but we have poachers and habitat encroachment for them.

Centrifuge: A device that uses rotational energy to separate mixtures into their respective parts by exploiting differences in their density. They work kind of like that ride at the county fair that spins and holds you up against the wall, except there is less vomit and there isn't a meth head operating it... probably.

Charles Guiteau: A wacky and eccentric man of God who was known in his day for a series of wild adventures. These included but were not limited to this impressive list of acheivements: joining a free-love commune that extoled the virtues of casual sex and the importance of female orgasms; leaving the same free-love commune after getting exactly zero "free-love" and being nicknamed "Charles Get-out"; failing the BAR exam and then becoming a lawyer anyway without telling anyone; marrying a librarian and then banging a hooker who later testified to Charles' infidelity so that he could get divorced (at his wife's request); surviving a boating accident and proclaiming that God had spared him from death so that he could do great things; writing a speech supporting James A. Garfield for president that no one asked him to deliver and then begging the newly elected President Garfield to appoint him as consul of Paris; and last but not least, buying an ivory handled Webley .442 revolver and assassinating president Garfield with it.

Cholera: The disease caused by *Vibrio cholerae* bacteria that is characterized by intense bouts of sustained diarrhea and vomiting. Exposure to drinking water or food contaminated with human feces is the primary cause of infection. Humans are the only known host for the *Vibrio* bacteria so you should feel special.

Cicada: The common name for species of insects belonging to the superfamily *Cicadoidea*. There are three thousand known species of cicada that are found all over the world. Cicadas are known for their complete metamorphic life cycle; distinctive long transparent wings, and impressive ability to not shut the fuck up for the entire summer; we get it!

Cinderella: Fictional character from European folklore whose name is translated from various forms of "little cinder girl" or "little ash girl". The story has many versions, but the overarching theme in each story is if you meet a monarch whom you might want to marry, you should say your name at least one time or give him your phone number before you leave him for the night. Similarly, if you are a monarch who has fallen madly in love with a girl who you have danced with for like five minutes, and you are willing to devote the entire country's resources to finding someone who fits into her glass slipper, you should not do that because it is insane. Also, be better with faces.

Clitoris: that little buttony thing right there at the top-middle part of the center of the vagina, maybe?

Chlamydia: A venereal disease caused by *Chlamydia trachomatis* bacteria. The infection is most often characterized by white or watery discharge from the cervix in women, or the tip of the penis in men. The strain of chlamydia found in wild koalas is not the same as the one found in humans but you can catch the koala version if one pees on you. Or presumably from having sex with one. To be on the safe side, and to avoid comitting a crime against nature, don't fuck a koala bear.

Cockroach: An insult uttered with much passion by the fictional character Tony Montana in the movie Scarface. Used both generally as "A man ain't got his word is a cock-a-roach" and specifically in reference to several drug dealer rivals. "Fuck Gaspar Gomez and fuck the fucking Diaz Brothers. Fuck 'em all. I bury those cock-a-roaches." Cockroach is also the name of a hardy group of insects in the order *Blattaria*.

Costis Mitsotakis: a Greek documentary filmmaker who is definitely not upset about being the only person in the town of Sodeto, Spain to not win a portion of the countries largest lottery prize.

Cymothoa exigua: The tongue-eating louse. A species of marine isopod that has a fetish for defecating down the throats of fish. To further this end, the louse eats the tongue of its host and latches down on the stub of flesh at the base of the mouth. This effectively replaces the tongue and allows the isopod to eat the fish's food and poop into the host fish's esophagus. The fetish part might not be true but unfortunately the rest is. Either way, the poop has to go somewhere right?

D

Dead in Absentia: A legal declaration made when a person is believed to be dead without any evidence of their remains being found. Examples of this include when a person is lost at sea or when your buddy doesn't show up to the hotel continental breakfast on the last day of the bachelor weekend after being last seen entering a lifted El Camino with two Peruvian acrobats and a "shaman."

Deforestation: The intentional clearing or thinning of trees that decreases the size of a forest. This totally sustainable practice sometimes receives critisicm because Earth is the only planet in the galaxy that has trees, and we have already removed 1/3 of them. Alarmists like to point out that this means the only planet that has trees is getting a "D" grade in having trees. Everyone else is too busy getting laid and burning things to pay any attention to that.

Democracy: A governmental system whereby people elect the people who will rob and cheat them rather than the much less preferred method of having no say in which leaders will rob and cheat them. Basically it is as good a system that could be produced by humans as long as you ask someone that does not live in one.

Dick move: A broad category of actions that would cause a reasonable person to assume you are an asshole. Examples: Taking three pieces of pizza when there are four people sharing an eight cut. Pulling the chair out from under a disabled child to watch them fall. Tea-bagging someone in Halo when you were shamelessly spawn-camping. Commiting genocide.

Dinosaur: An excellent insult for anyone one generation or more your elder. An even better insult for someone who is only slightly older than you and very insecure. A group of prehistoric terrestrial reptiles that dominated the Earth from 245 to 65 million years ago.

Dog: The common name for the species *Canis lupus familiaris*. A domesticated sub-species of the grey wolf that has been associated with humans for at least twelve thousand years. I imagine the grey wolves would rather just be left out of the discussion rather than be lumped in the same family as pugs and miniature poodles.

Dr. Karl P. Schmidt: An American Herpetologist who was born on June 19, 1890, and died September 26, 1957. Dr. Schmidt contributed greatly to ecological theory and animal classification. His work advanced our understanding of reptile and amphibian taxonomy and evolution. Despite his enormous contributions to zoology, he is most remembered for fatally mishandling a snake and writing about the effects rather than seeking medical treatment.

Drone: An unmanned flying vehicle that is controlled remotely or a male honeybee. One of them may be armed with Hellfire missiles and sophisticated surveillance equipment and the other is a harmless garden insect. It is difficult to tell the difference, so beware.

Dysentery: An disease of the intestines that can be acquired by ingesting feces containing either bacteria of the *Shigella* genus or the protozoan *Entamoeba histolytica*, the first of which causes bacillary dysentery, while the latter causes amebic dysentery. In either version, the symptoms are similar. You spew diarrhea and blood out of your ass until you die of dehydration.

E

Earth: The third planet from the star at the center of our solar system. The planet you are currently residing on and the only planet yet discovered that harbors living things. It is also the only planet with pedophilia and imitation crab meat so don't get too proud, humanity.

Emerald jewel wasp: The common name for *Ampulex compressa*, a solitary parasitic wasp of the family *Ampulicidae*. All species in this family use living cockroaches to feed their developing larva. (See "Dick move" under the D heading above.)

Emperor penguin: The largest and heaviest living penguin. Scientific name: *Aptenodytes forsteri*. This arrogant, formally dressed, flightless bird is proof that humans aren't the only creatures guilty of living in places where they have no business being (Sahara Desert, the bases of active volcanoes, next to golf courses).

Estrogen: A group of sex hormones responsible for regulating the reproductive systems of females and the expression of secondary sex characteristics. It is also responsible for the continued success of HGTV, Starbucks iced coffee and misogyny. Sorry, ladies, if there were no women there could be no sexism. So you see, it is your fault.

Estrus: The technical term for "going into heat." The point of the menstrual cycle in which a female becomes sexually receptive. In many animals there are outward physical changes marking estrus, such as, reddening of the labia, swelling of the genitals, and elevation of the hind quarters. In humans it is mainly characterized by spontaneous text messages saying "You up?"

Eucalyptus tree: The name given to about seven hundred different flowering trees in the myrtle family (Myrtaceae). The trees are mainly found in Australia and proved just how inflammable they are when the entire continent burned down in 2019.

European colonizers: Bastards who ruined everything, according to the Aztec priest who was carving the still-beating heart out of a prisoner of war so that the Sun would rise the next day.

Evolution: A bunch of malarky about how sexual selection and environmental pressures influence the traits and adaptions of a species to the point of forming new species over the course of long stretches of time.

F

Fahrenheit: A unit of temperature measuremenet that is used in the Fahrenheit scale invented by Daniel Gabriel Fahrenheit in 1724. Though this scale has been largely abandoned in favor of the Celcius scale, it was a major improvement on previous systems of measuring things as cold, cool, warm, hot, and OW!

Ferret: Species of small, carnivorous mammal of the family *Mustelidae*. Other mustelids include weasels, polecats, badgers, and minks. Ferrets put the "must" in Mustelidae because females "must" get laid or they will die.

Finding Nemo: A Disney and Pixar produced animated film that ends in the titular character Nemo being flushed down a drain that leads directly to the ocean and ultimately to his father who has been looking for him. This ending is ridiculous because the drain is part of a commercial plumbing fixture in a dentist's office. As such, it would lead to some kind of waste water treatment facility unlike storm drains, which take rain runoff and surface water to aquifers such as the ocean. A more adequate ending would show young Nemo being eviscerated in some sort of strainer before his liquified remains were sanitized and filtered out of the now potable sewer water. Also, I do not believe that fish can talk, so that's also a bit unrealistic, if you ask me.

Final Destination: A supernatural horror movie franchise first appearing on screen in the year 2000 that is responsible for irrational fears of driving behind logging trucks, using tanning salons, riding county fair roller coasters and sitting in single lane fast-food drive-throughs

Free-swimming penis impersonator: Another name for the sea cucumber first popularized by the author of this book.

G

German/Germany German is something or someone belonging to, hailing from, or associated with the country of Germany. Germany is a country in central Europe that was officially formed in 1866 from the union of twenty-three smaller states. Germany is the second most populous country in Europe after Russia and the world's 4th largest economy. The country also hold the twentieth century's award for "biggest shit-mixer" after those two little scraps in the first half of the 1900s.

G- Force A specific phenomenon wherein an accelerating object experiences the force of gravity acting upon it from the opposite direction of their acceleration. Also a brand of watch so named because it has a similar effect on consumers. You approach the watch display and see the G-Force watch and you feel a force pushing you in the opposite direction of the ridiculous-looking timepiece.

Giant panda bear: Also called giant panda or panda bear. These names refer to the species *Ailuropoda melanoleuca*. A true bear that is endemic to China and nowhere else. The term "giant panda" is thought to differentiate the panda from the so-called red panda, which is not a bear or related to giant pandas at all. It is actually a mustelid more closely related to badgers. Despite this being known for decades, we just keep calling them red panda bears because scientists are lazy, and the public is dumb. Lazy and dumb are perfect descriptors for actual pandas because they would rather munch on bamboo all day than eat the meat their bodies were designed for.

Greek/Greece: Greek is something or someone belonging to, hailing from or associated with the country of Greece. Greek also is the official language spoken in Greece. Greece (officially the Hellenic Republic) is a European country located on the southern tip of the Balkan Peninsula. Greece is the birthplace of democracy, Western philosophy, Western literature, Western politics, the gyro and correcting people on the proper pronunciation of the word gyro.

God or god: The perfect prefix for the word "damn" and also a term representing specific supernatural dieties in many religions. When capitialized it typically refers to the creator of the universe in the Abrahamic religions of Judiasm, Cristianity, and Islam.

George Washington: The first president of the United States of America, commander of the Continental Army, founding father, author, and statesman. Probably not jazzed that everybody's favorite trivia bit about him involves his dentures.

Guillaume Hyacinthe Jean-Baptiste Le Gentil de la Galasaisier: Astronomer famous for not seeing a celestial event. That is kind of like me being famous for never having seen Zeppelin in concert. I'm bummed that I never got the chance but it isn't really newsworthy.

H

Harlequinn crab: The common name for *Lissocarcinus orbicularis*, a species of commensal symbiote that feeds on the tissue of the sea cucumbers that it lives on or inside of. Because the sea cucumber can easily regenerate its tissue without adverse effects and because it liekly has no knowledge of the harm even happening due to its lack of pain receptors, the clearly parasitic harlequin crab is not labelled as such. Apparently there is a "no harm, no foul" clause when catagorizing symbiotic relationships.

Hermaphrodite: An organism posessing both male and female reproductive organs. This is usually the specific species' normal body plan but can also appear as a genetic mutation in other organisms. In humans it can be viewed as a taboo condition but I gotta say it would make dating a lot easier if you had access to the entire pool of eligible humans regardless of what they are packing.

Hiroo Onoda: Japanese soldier during WWII and undisputed champion of hide and seek... ...ing out villages to raid.

HOA: An acronym for Homeowner's Association. This godless, joyless assemblage of people who would rather preserve the collective property value of their neighborhood through inquisitorial tattling, pettiness, and asinine rules than minding their own fucking business.

Honeybee: The collective name for the eight different species of honey producing bees around the world. In the United States and Europe, the most common of these is the European honey bee *Apis mellifera*.

I

Illuminati: A secret society first called the Bravarian Illuminati, founded in 1776 by Adam Weishaupt. The groups stated goal was "...To put an end to the machinations of the purveyors of injustice, to control them without dominating them." Ironically, the group aimed to oppose superstition, obscurantism, and the abuses of state power. It is ironic because they are almost completely known for partaking in all of those things in popular culture and conspiracy theories.

Isopod: Any of the ten thousand species of the order isopoda, a branch of crustacaens that can be aquatic or terrestrial. This group includes the wood louse, sow bug, and tongue-eating parasitic nightmare fuel.

J

James A. Garfield: The twentieth president of the United States of America and a lauded civil rights advocate. He probably would have lived longer had he been a washing-your-filthy-fucking-hands-before-surgery advocate. Garfield was also a skilled mathematician who published a proof of the Pythagorem theorum which makes him the nerdiest president to be assasinated.

Japan: Country in the South Pacific that is the world's third largest economy and also the only country where you can buy used panties in a vending machine. Japan is the birthplace of anime, Toyota, mass radiation poisoning and the fifth worst Fast & Furious movie.

Juniper Tre: The common juniper, a widespread tree in the Cupressaceae family (cypresses). It is an evergreen with transpolar distribution and distinctive blue fruits. They are used in the flavoring of gin. The Juniper Tree is also the name of a horror story for children collected by the Brothers Grimm.

K

Kanye West: An award-winning American rapper, songwriter, producer, and fashion designer who was born in Atlanta, Georgia on June 8, 1977. Kanye has sold twenty-one million albums and won critical acclaim for his groundbreaking style and musical skills. He also suffered a very public mental breakdown and was diagnosed with schitzophrenia but he was also married to Kim Kardashian for eight years, so that may not have been avoidable.

Kidnapping: A crime defined as abducting, forcefully moving, or imprisoning a person, usually for ransom. Comes from the words "kid" and "nab" meaning to grab.

Kim Kardashian: World's most successful single-credit porn star who married Chris Humphries before divorcing him seventy-two days later. Also probably the richest person to ever fail the BAR exam.

Kiwi bird: A species of bird of the genus *Apteryx*. The kiwi bird is the smallest member of the ratite family, whom the inhabitants of the island of New Zealand are named after. Also where the kiwi fruit gets its name from due to its similar appearance to a bird which is ridiculous but true.

Knots: A unit of speed equal to one nautical mile per hour or exactly 1.852 km/h. Used extensively to measure the speed of boats and aircraft. It gets its name from the original way of measuring the speed of vessels at sea using a movement resistant piece of weighted wood called a chip log and a length of string with knots tied in it every forty-seven feet and three inches.

Sailors would record the number of knots that passed through their hands in a thirty second period as speed of the vessel in knots.

Koala bear: The common and taxonomically misleading name for *Phascolarctos cinereus,* a species of marsupial native to Australia and owner of the world's smoothest mammal brain so the only way it could get dumber is if it were a fish or a lizard or something.

L

Laboratory rat: A truly unfortunate domesticated subspecies of rat bred from wild rats of the species *Rattus norvegicus* for the purpose of research and testing. There are two major sub groups of laboratory rats. "Strains" refer to inbred populations of rats that are created to represent specific disorders or to rule out genetic variation in testing. "Stocks" are populations of outbred rats that are used when gene variation is not a factor or where genetic diversity is required. Some rats are even specifically bred to have 100 percent chance of dying from genetic disorders. This is done so that as the rats die of painful degenerative disorders so we can study them. This practice is better than using people because rats have not evolved a way to say "Ow".

Laika: The first dog to die in space. Also the first dog to visit space, which is usually how she is attributed but to-may-toe to-mah-toe she was the first to do both.

Leucochloridium paradoxum: A parasitic flatworm that infects certain snail species for the purpose of using the snail's eye as a vehicle to enter the GI tract of a bird. Of note: this flatworm is not very flat and not very wormy and also an asshole.

LiveLeak: A free media-hosting site based in Britian that was founded in October of 2006 and remained active until 2021. The founder, Hayden Hewitt, aimed to host real footage of world events involving politics and war. LiveLeak gained notoriety as a place to view and post graphic and violent content, which eventually led to its downfall. An entire generation of

Internet users remember Liveleak as the place they saw their first behead-ing video after being sent a link to such videos with absolutely zero context, this author included.

Lottery: A way to raise money through the drawing of numbers that corro-spond to a prepurchased ticket or receipt. An even dumber way of earning money than writing a morbid motivational guide.

Lungfish: A group of fish in the class Dipnoi that can breathe atmospheric oxygen and seal themselves in a mucus condom for long stretches at a time. Lungfish may not be as flashy as marlins or popular as salmon but they are disgusting, bottom feeding losers that spend most of their time lying motionless at the bottom of seasonal rivers and the rest of the time in sus-pended animation so they have that going for them.

M

Mammary glands: A type of apocrine gland found in all mammals that is specialized for the production and secretion of milk for the purposes of feeding offspring. The milk itself is produced inside apocrine cells that first fill with the substance, then explode, releasing the milk along with debris from the destroyed cell. In a way, all mammal infants are obligate canni-bals. Mammary glands in humans are sometimes referred to in scientific literature as boobs, tits, fun bags, sweater pillows, and ta-tas among other less politically correct terminology.

Malaria: A disease caused by contact with one of five species of single-celled plasmodia. Malaria is spread through the bite of about one hundred differ-ent species of *Anopheles* mosquito. Malaria is the all-time leading cause of death of humans over the course of the species' existence, killing an estimated 5 percent of all humans who have ever lived (5.54 billion peo-ple). The genus of mosquito responsible for transmitting the disease gets its name from the Greek words for "useless" and "profit." The name is less fitting today, when the global anti-malarial drug market is worth 711 mil-lion dollars.

Mansplaining: Ladies, for some reason I can't quite place my fingers on, I feel like you need this broken down into simpler terms. Mansplaining is an ingeniously crafted strategy that aims to place a negative connotation on describing or clarifying one's point. It is thought that human females introduced the idea that explaining a quandry, process or motivation to someone for the purpose of edifying them is condescending to the person whom the information is being presented to. In this way, a stigma is placed on passing information proactively and the chances of being educated by the males of the species is reduced over time.

MapQuest: A free web-mapping service first founded in 1996 in Lancaster, Pennsylvania. While revolutionary at the time, it is funny to think back to a time before smartphones and GPS, when instead of being distracted by your car's HUD, you read lined directions from a stack of papers, which completely obscured your view of the road.

Marsupial: The organisms belonging to the mammalian infraclass Marsupialia. The members of this group cannot produce a placenta and carry their developing young in an external pouch. Most well-known marsupial species are found in Australia, such as kangaroos, koalas, and wombats. The Virginia opposum is the only North-American marsupial. In their native range, opposum are most often seen as flattened corpses on the side of roads. However, they can also be observed as hideous, fear-paralyzed balls of fluff on top of garbage cans.

Masturbation: The act of sexually pleasuring one self by manipulating the genitals or surrounding tissue, usually performed in private but sometimes with witnesses. In the latter cases, the witness is usually aroused or horrified depending on the context of their participation. Masturbation is generally enjoyable, can relieve stress, release endorphins, and can benefit prostate health, so naturally, it is almost universally considered taboo and is forbidden in most religions.

Masturbating Man of Pompeii: An unknown victim of the volcanic eruption that destroyed the ancient Roman city of Pompeii. He appears, at least superficially, to be preserved in ash in the act of sexually gratifying himself. To be fair, he probably wasn't thinking about the chances that he would one day be on display at a musuem while he was rubbing one out to the end of the world.

Matriarchal: A society or group in which the mother or oldest female is the defacto leader and/or the lines of ascension to power run through the female members of the group. I normally end these definitions with a joke, but I will not lower myself to such juvenile pretenses that dominate gender-based humor. Instead, I will simply state that humans are the only non matriarchal primates and also the only primates who can parallel park a car.

McDonalds: A multinational fast-food franchise started in San Bernedino County in 1940. Today McDonald's is the world's second largest private employer and operates or owns forty thousand franchises in over one hundred countries. In 1999, my twin brother got a Nidoking Pokemon in his McDonald's Happy Meal and I got a Poliwag and I have never forgiven McDonald's for that. Fuck you, Ronald.

Meteorite: A piece of solid debris that originates in outer space and survives its passage through the atmosphere and onto the surface of a celestial body. In astronomical terms, a bolide is a meteorite large enough to leave an impact crater. In mathematical terms, the chances of being struck by a meteorite are approximately one in all-of-numbers-since-the-dawn-of-time because that's the only time it has happened. That statement is "true" in the sense that "approximately" just means "close to," and an infinite number of numbers means that every number is the same distance away from every other number on a line, so every possible numerical answer for a given question is approximately correct.

Michael Malloy: A homeless ex-firefighter and Irish immigrant who lived in New York City during the 1920s and 1930s. Michael Malloy was murdered by a group of five conspirators after the same group had failed on dozens of previous attempts to kill him via alcohol poisoning, food poisoning, regular old poisoning, exposure, and blunt force trauma via vehicular assault.

Miller: A person who owns or works at a grain mill for the purpose of turning cereal crops into flour. Miller is the most popular Amish surname and seventh most popular surname among the general population in America. Miller is also the actual surname of a man my old boss used to call "Marvin Yoder" because he thought that all Amish people have the last name Yoder.

Mola mola: A ray-finned fish species of the family Molidae. Also called an ocean sunfish. They are the largest ray-finned fish and also one of the most made-up looking creatures in the same oceans that have sawtooth sharks, cuttlefish, and megalodons (maybe).

Moscow: A city in Central Europe that is the capitol of the Russian Federation and home to thirteen million people. Moscow is the largest city in Europe and the sixth-largest city in the world. Moscow is also home to the world's most edible-looking church in St. Basil's Cathedral.

N

Nemo: [see Finding Nemo page 180]

New Zealand: An island nation off the coast of Australia that was the last large land mass to be settled by humans. It is believed that Homo sapiens did not arrive on the islands of New Zealnd until around 1280 AD. Because of the relatively late colonization by people, the new natives had a lot of catching up to do in the "hunting animals to exinction and spoiling the environment" department. They caught up pretty quick though.

Norway: A Nordic country in Northen Europe that comprises the westernmost and northern parts of the Scandanavian Peninsula. Norway has employed an officer of the King's Guard in a permanent post at the Edinburgh Zoo in Scotland since 1972. The office is in the zoo because Brigadier Sir Nils Olav III is a penguin which is somehow true.

O

Octopus: Any of the three hundred species of eight limbed mollusks of the order Octopoda. These incredible creatures are known for their high intellegence, excellent camoflage, mimcry skills, and their sub-par ability to play the clarinet.

Orca: A toothed marine mammal of the Delphinidea family. Often called a "killer whale" even though it is an oceanic dolphin. The orca is found in every ocean and across all climates and is usually the apex predator in its given range. The orcas' complex language of clicks and whistles, which is often unique to particular family groups has been proposed as an example of animal culture. Despite claims of this supposed culture, there has never been a recorded case of an orca properly setting a table for a formal meal service. It goes dinner knife, salad knife then soup spoon on the far right you imbeciles!

Ornithologist: A scientist who studies birds. An amatuer ornithologist is an extremely generous term for a person in their fifties who has taken up bird watching and owns a pair of binoculars.

Osama Bin Laden: Full name Osama bin Mohammed bin Awad bin Laden was a Saudi Arabian-born soldier and terrorist leader who formed the terror group Al Queda and planned the September 11 attacks on the United States. After his assassination in 2011, it was found that besides being a stone cold killer and violent idealogue, Bin Laden also had an extensive collection of anime cartoons which sounds fake but is true.

Osmosis Jones: The titular character in the 2001 animation movie starring Chris Rock and Bill Murray as a white blood cell cop and the body he is protecting, respectively. The movie was and remains an absolute masterpiece albiet one that was critically panned and lost fifty-four million dollars.

P

Parasite/parasitic/parasitism: An organism that lives on or inside of another organism and who derives some or all of its energy from that organism to the detriment of the organism itself. An example of this is how Ticketmaster leeches money out of consumers by latching onto live entertainment acts and forcing them to use Ticketmaster to disseminate tickets. Fifty-five fucking dollars of fees on a seventy-five dollar ticket? Ticketmaster, you are the devil.

Pearlfish: Yes, yes, a fish that lives inside a sea cucumber's ass.

Penis: The male sex organ of almost all mammals, some birds, some reptiles, and certain invertebrates. The penis is primarily used for the transmission of sperm during copulation. In placental mammals, the penis is also how urine is expelled through the body. The penis is also the source of approximately 78 percent of all humor in human adolescent males.

Penguin: A recurring, bird-themed villian in the DC Comic Universe who has appeared in print, television, and film. Also a group of semi-aquatic birds who have received the worst evolutionary trade deal in the history of trade deals. They traded flying- which all birds can do -for swimming which most birds can also already do while still being able to fly. Stupid.

Philanthropist: A person who funds charitable causes through significant monetary contributions because they care about the welfare of others. … and also tax write-offs. …and also getting their name on things. …and also their "legacy" which is rich people talk for "people not openly talking about how much of an asshole I was."

Philippines: Officially, the Republic of the Philippines is a nation of 7,641 islands in the South Pacific Ocean. It is the twelfth most populous nation in the world and the seventh most populous nation in Asia. The fifty-sixth most valuable export of the Philippines is electric hair dryers.

Pill bug: A colloquial name for several species of terrestrial isopods sometimes also called roly-polys. Pill bug is also a pejoritive name given by some insects to other insects who are either known to be or suspected to be opiate addicts.

Placenta: An organ that forms around the developing fetus of placental mammals. This organ simultaneously creates a barrier around, and passageway to, the fetus from the mother's womb. The placenta supplies nutrients to, expels waste from, and insulates the fetus throughout pregnancy. Imagine a bloody sneeze and the mucus that it would produce. Then imagine that expectorant is large enough for a baby to develop inside of. Now completely cover the bloody snot ball with blood vessels, and you have accurately pictured a placenta.

Poison: Any substance that can harm or kill an organism who ingests or otherwise metabolizes that substance. Although often used interchangeably with the word venom, poison is a distinctly different substance from venom. Whereas Poison is an American glam metal band formed in 1983 in Mechanicsburg, Pennsylvania, Venom is a British thrash/black metal band formed in 1978 in Newcastle Upon Tyne in England.

Pondicherry: Apparently not a place anymore. It is still a place, but it is called Puducherry which I think is less fun to say. Puducherry is a city in Southeast India that probably had an incredibly interesting and long history before Europeans showed up and "started" recording history there in 1521.

Porn: An image, movie, or written work that portrays sexual activity, usually explicit but sometimes implied. Pornography accounts for anywhere from 4 percent to fifteen percent of the entire Internet, which is actually down from the 40 percent of total Internet content in 1999. It is worth noting that the volume of porn on the Internet has not gone down, it has risen exponentially. There is not less porn now than in 1999 there is just more of everything else. Also worth noting, porn is the third biggest reason that this book has taken so long to finish.

Prius: A revolutionary hybrid and fully electric car built by Toyota Motors that was the first commercially successful electric vehicle. Also the second most mocked vehicle of all time by men between the ages of twenty and eighty-five.

Prohibition: A terrible idea that materialized in the passage of the eighteenth amendment to the United States Constitution prohibiting the sale or consumption of alcohol at the federal level. The only positive thing to come from prohibition was that once sober, the country realized they had made an oopsie and forgotten to give women the right to vote. The nineteenth amendment rectified that mistake by protecting women's right to vote. The twentieth amendment rectified the mistake of banning alcohol by repealing the eighteenth amendment and once sufficiently liquored up again, men have not listened to women about anything since.

Pseudo-penis: A pretty gnarly band name that I'm almost certain is still available if you are in the market. Also, the name of the organ that extends from the female hyena's vagina. So named because it looks pretty much exactly like a weiner.

PT Cruiser: The first most mocked vehicle of all time.

Q

Quadruped: Any animal that has four legs. Note that while they do technically fit that description, spiders are not quadrupeds. Think Horse.

R

Rape: In humans, is a heinous and depraved crime involving forcing sexual penetration on another human. In many animals it is just kind of how the cookie crumbles. And by "cookie" I mean babies, and by "crumbles" I mean get made.

Ratite: A family of flightless birds that includes the ostriches, cassowaries and rhea. Has nothing to do with rats.

Ray J: The real architect behind the Kardashian family fortune.

Rectum: Coming from the latin phrase *rectum intestinum* meaning "straight intestine" the rectum is the final portion of the GI tract in humans and other mammals and also a recurring food item on the show Fear Factor for some goddamn reason.

Roadkill: A term for the most common outcome of an interaction between my wife and any wildlife within a fifty square-mile radius of our home.

Roald Amundsen: A Norwegian explorer born on July 16, 1872 who led the first successful expedition to the South Pole and whose most popular portrait looks suspiciously like the bad guy from the Saw movies. That comparison is more than coincidental when you read about how he sustained himself and his dogs during his polar expedition. "Fido, I want to play a game with you."

Robber Bridegroom: Not how you want to be introduced at your wedding reception. Also a horrific folkstory in the horrific collection of folkstories told by the horrific Brothers Grimm.

Robert Falcon Scott: A british explorer who died during his attempt to be the first person to reach the South Pole. Probably really could have used a Twix bar toward the end there.

Robert Todd Lincoln: Basically the grim reaper of presidential guests. He was present at the shooting of or visited with three US presidents after their shootings. The first of these shootings was his father Abraham Lincoln, who you may remember from his association with log-shaped building blocks.

Rosemary's Baby: A 1968 horror movie based on a novel of the same name in which a young woman becomes pregnant and starts freaking out for no reason. IDK; I didn't watch the whole thing.

Roy Sullivan: Nicknamed "the human lightning rod" or "Jesus, Roy, get out of the rain! Don't you ever learn?" Roy Sullivan still holds the record for the individual who has been struck by lightning the most times. He was struck seven times in his life which is seven more than most people and six more than most people who are extremely careless around thunderstorms.

RuneScape: If you were eleven years old, RuneScape was the coolest thing you could do on your computer in 2005 that did not involve lubrication. RuneScape is a free-to-play MMORPG-style video game that was first released in 2001. The game features a variety of fantasy-based character development branches and features quests and monsters and all kinds of nerdy shit like that. It was nice while it lasted, sadly being shut down forever in… Holy dog shit, RuneScape is still a thing?! It has over two million players in any given twenty-four hour period?! That is bananas!

Russia/Russian: A country spanning much of Northern Europe and Asia, the largest country by area and the world's most prolifically armed nuclear power. In Russia the national anthem is the creatively named "State Anthem of the Russian Federation". In the United States the official anthem of Russia is the soundtrack to the 1997 Nintendo 64 game Goldeneye.

S

Scrote: An immature and totally rad slang term for nutsack.

Schmuck: A Yiddish term for my lawyer. To be clear, it does not actually mean "my lawyer," but it does work in every instance of someone trying to describe their lawyer.

Sea Cucumbe: 100 percent the worst-tasting vegetable in the world and one of the hardest to grow in your backyard.

Self-destructing balls: A fitting if non-scientific term for the genitals of male honeybees. So called (by me) because they explode fatally during intercourse.

Sex: A type of reproduction in living organisms that requires genes from more than one parent. I saw more than one because although sexual reproduction involves two parents in most cases, of course there has to be some exceptions. At least one kind of salamander and lots of plants can have three biological parents. In the context where it appears here, sex is a term used by humans to describe sexual intercourse usually involving humans but not always. This is more precisely described as "when the pee-pee goes

airplane noises down into the vi-jay-jay and little babies are made". Sex can also be used to describe different types of gamete producing organisms within the same species. I wish I could be more specific but I'm not sure what the rules on what you can and can't say about sex and gender are going to be at the time of reading and I don't want to get cancelled. Whatever you think sex is, is correct and I support you.

Siberian pony: A cold-adapted stocky horse breed native to Yakutia (Siberia). They have very thick and long hair and can tolerate extremely cold weather. Nineteen of these unfortunate beasts were taken to and ultimately died in Antarctica in 1911 aboard Robert Falcon Scott's doomed *Terra Nova* expedition. The ponies did accomplish something rather impressive though; they managed to be the first and probably last horses to be eaten by orcas.

Shitsicle: A formed stool that, being expelled in a sufficiently cold environment, freezes [traditionally] while still being excreted. In less strict definitions a shitsicle can also freeze upon contact with the frozen ground once dropped. A sort of stalagtite, stalagmite distinction, if you will.

Skin-Flute: An incredibly disturbing wind instrument used by cannibals during certain religious ceremonies or at the commencement of a feast. I'm kidding; it is a slang term for penis. I mean... ... I guess it could be both but I really hope not.

Sleeping Beauty: The protagonist from a series of folkstories and later Disney properties of the same name who I suppose was just called "Beauty" until she pricked her finger. Ope, nevermind, her name is apparently Aurora. I mean it's not like they could just name the poor girl after her physical description. That would be ridiculous.

Snow White: The protagonist from a series of folkstories and later Disney properties of the same name whose actual name really is Snow White. No shit; they saw that she was pale as an infant and called her "Schneewittchen" which translates to Snow Fucking White without the "Fucking" part.

South Pole Skua: A predatory bird that is roughly the size of a sea gull that prefers to steal food from other birds or just steal the bird's children rather than hunt for themselves.

Soviet scientist: The basic unit of henchman needed to create a pre-1990 James Bond movie, a third tier Marvel villain or anything with Steven Seagal in it. Also the nerds responsible for beating the US to every space race milestone except the big one. Suck it, Ruskies!

Spain: A Western European nation in the Iberian Peninsula that borders France to the east and Portugal to the west. Also the place where the Spanish language originated, which would surprise many of my neighbors who are pissed at the Mexicans for ruining what they call "Anglish".

Spotted hyenas: The oddly fascistic pack hunters who made up the bulk of Scar's army in The Lion King. Also the apex predators in the real African Savannah who would have chewed Scar's old, malnourished rusty-looking hide to pieces the moment he started singing "Be Prepared."

S.S. Arctic: A steam powered, side paddle ocean liner that sank off the coast of Newfoundland in 1854, causing the deaths of 315 people. Most of the victims were women and children because chivalry actually died a long, long time ago.

SS Princess Alice: A British passenger steam ship that sank in the Thames River in 1878, causing the deaths of 600-700 passengers. The only thing worse than living in London during the Industrial Revolution was dying in the toxic waste that it produced. This is exactly what happened to the hapless souls when they were tossed into the putrid effluent coming from London's sewers the moment they sank.

S.T.D.: The acronym for Sexually Transmitted Disease. A diverse class of infectious diseases that can be contracted through sexual contact. These pathogens are so prevalent because viruses and bacteria figured out long ago that people would literally rather die of AIDS than stop boning.

S.T.E.M.: The acronym for Science, Technology, Engineering and Mathematics. It is a descriptor for some of the most necessary fields in the sciences and also some of the most likely majors to not have to worry about contracting an STD. Not because they are smart enough to use a condom, but because they are nerdy enough to not get a chance to use them.

Stepsiste: A female sibling related through marriage rather than genetics. Also the fastest growing sub-genre of pornography for some fucked-up reason.

Sun: The thing that hurts your eyes when you look at the brightest part of the sky during the daytime. Also a burning ball of super dense gases around ninty-three million miles from Earth that will eventually supernova and destroy our solar system. Not to worry, humanity will have gone extinct long before that happens.

T

Tasmanian devil: Scientific name, *Sarcophilus harrisii*. A carnivorous marsupial native to the islands of Tasmania off the coast of New Zealand. Not actually a spinning, slobbering brownish oaf of a cartoon character. Well, I guess it is also that but "Taz" looks nothing like his real-life brother. He is missing the face tumors, the horrible stench and he is not shoulders deep in the rotting asshole of some roadkill.

Terra Nova: A coal-burning, single screw, three-masted whaling-barque-turned expedition-vessel that famously carried Robert Falcon Scott and his crew on their South Pole Expedition in 1910. The ship returned quite a bit lighter than it had departed as it was without nineteen horses, various sled dogs, a motor sledge and five of the crew who all died or were lost during the "successful" expedition.

Testicle: The male reproductive gland that appears in all bilateral animals including humans (minus politicians and phone scammers). Testicles are responsible for producing sperm and testosterone along with other androgen hormones. Testicle is also the thirteenth funniest word in the English language.

Testosterone: That stuff that makes you want to punch a wall when you are angry at minor inconveniences or physically dominate another person at a completely inappropriate moment for the sole purpose of getting a female's attention. Can be replaced by purchasing a motor vehicle with excessive horsepower or by taking steroids.

TMZ: Just the saddest group of "journalists."

Thomas Midgley Jr.: An American chemist and inventor who synthesized the first leaded anti-knock compound, the first CFC based refrigerant, and a pretty sub-par manlift.

Transit of Venis: A phenomenon visible with the aid of a telescope in which the planet Venus passes in front of the Sun and appears as a black dot moving across the Solar surface. By calculating the difference in angles between the Earth and the Sun and Venus and the Sun, it was thought that one could surmise the size of the entire solar system. Astronomers from all over the world studied the transit of Venus during multiple sightings and determined the size of the Solar System within 2 percent of the generally accepted value today. That is, astronomers from all over the world except one from France who failed to see either of the transits that happened in his life time due to some extremely bad luck.

Tree: You don't know what a fucking tree is?

TSA: The Transportation Security Administration. A branch of the American Department of Homeland Security created after the September 11 terrorist attacks in the United States. TSA is responsible for all transportation systems throughout or connecting to the United States. TSA is also basically the opposite of a convenience store. If it makes your life easier, they are not about it.

Turtle formation: A protective formation of emporer penguins that has nothing to do with turtles because of course it is. Fuck you scientists, you suck at naming things.

U

Universe: Everything.

Unpaid intern: A type of Schrodinger's individual in that they are someone who is getting screwed a lot but is also probably not getting screwed a lot. A strange type of employment that involves forcing someone to work for school credit instead of money. It is strange because the promise of using the unpaid interning skills to make yourself more employable someday is somewhat misleading. Companies don't pay salaried employees to do the work of unpaid interns, they get unpaid interns to do it. So, what is your work experience really worth?

U.S. government: The largest employer of leeches, snakes, jackals, cockroaches and clowns outside of the zoo. (Do zoos have clowns? Are clowns people?) Also the caretakers of approx. four thousand nuclear weapons, 1.3 million active duty military personnel and four hundred F-35 Joint Strike Fighters.

U.S.S. Indianapolis: An American Portland-class heavy cruiser launched in 1931. It served during WWII and famously delivered the uranium and other components needed to make the atomic bomb that was dropped on Hiroshima in 1945. After successfully delivering its payload, the Indianapolis was struck by a Japanese torpedo and sank, killing 879 sailors and marines.

U.S.S.R./Soviets: Union of Soviet Socialist Republics. A now disbanded transnational group of countries that were governed and controlled by its largest member state, Soviet Russia. Sort of like how the Coca Cola "family" is actually just Coca Cola and five hundred brands of other shit that they own in order to maintain their market dominance. ...Still better than Pepsi. (The U.S.S.R that is.)

V

Vagina: The muscular passage between the outer genitals and the uterus in human females and most other mammals. A word that must be searched for with safe search on if you want to see anything with research value. Also a term that appears in this book on half as many occasions as the word "penis". The goddamn patriarchy never rests.

Vegan: See "**vagina**". I'm sorry, that is a cheap shot. Vegans are people who do not consume animal derived foods and often do not use animal derived products, clothing, or cosmetics and that is perfectly fine. There is nothing wrong with an honorable if not misplaced desire to limit the harm your existence causes others. Just know that agriculture on any scale harms local fuana and disrupts the landscape, the avocados you like so much are basically the blood diamonds of Latin America and every time you shape tofu into the shape of some kind of meat an angel loses her wings mid-flight. The first two are true, the last one is just how I fell about tofu. Anytime somcone has to say, "it is good if you cook it right" in dcfcnsc of a food item, you should avoid that food.

Venom: Any substance produced by an animal with the intended purpose of harming another organism by way of entering that organism's blood stream through injection or absorbsion. Also the title of the 2018 movie featuring Tom Hardy's worst performance to date. (This was through no fault of his own; Marvel Studio had already started its fastideous decline into oversaturated garbage).

Venus: The second planet from the Sun in our Solar System, Venus is so inhospitable that no probe has survived more than two hours on its surface due to crushing pressure (ninety-two times more than on the Earth at sea level) and intense surface temperature of 890 degrees F. Add onto that the lack of breathable oxygen, no liquid water, and planet wide sulfuric acid storms it is no wonder that Venus is named for the Roman goddess of love and beauty.

Vibrator: A sex-toy that uses an oscillating electric motor to produce a pulsating motion for the purposes of sexual gratification and one of the least necessary inclusions to this glossary.

W

Warren G. Harding: The twenty-ninth president of the United States and definitely the president with the hardest to guess middle name. (Gamaliel) A close second would be Harry S Truman whose middle name is "S." Seriously it is just the letter.

William McKinley: The twenty-fifth president of the United States with absolutely no ties to Alaska, where a random-ass prospector from Seattle named the tallest mountain on the continent after him to commemorate his winning of the Republication nomination for president in 1896. Congress adopted the name officially twenty years after McKinely's assassination. In 2015, the name was changed to something that actually made sense, Denali. A name used by Native Americans in the region for hundreds of years.

Wilmer McLean: Born May 3, 1841, Wilmer was a wholesale grocer from Virginia whose houses (yes, two separate houses) were involved in the first and last battles of the American Civil War.

Windchill: A way to measure the perceived temperature drop and increased heat loss from a body or object as caused by the wind blowing over or across it. A common saying in the Midwestern United States is something to the effect of, "It wouldn't be that bad if it wasn't for the wind." Which is both a true and false statement when it is -3 degrees.

Winter: The season wherein a hemisphere of the planet is tilted away from the sun in such a way as to produce shortened daylight hours, colder temperatures and often increased precipitation. It is also the point where the bellies of most people are tilted toward the floor as people spend more time indoors, eating to combat boredom.

World Wildlife Fund: A great organization with a stupid mascot. Please don't sue me; I bought one of your plush toys when I went to the zoo last year.

WWII: An abbreviation for World War Two; the most destructive conflict in the history of the world. WWII was fought between 1939 and 1945 and involved nearly every country on Earth, with 127 million people being mobilized to fight and seventy-eight million lives lost. It was also the setting for the phenomenal first Call of Duty game so there is a small silver lining.

Y

You: The reader of this book. An individual who is likely very relieved to be on the last page. Who are we kidding? No one is going to read through an entire glossary except the editor, who was grossly underpayed to proofread this thing.

X

I don't have an entry for "X" but I did type "X is for" into Google Images and there were nineteen results on the first page that stated that "x is for X-mas tree". X-mas is of course an abbreviation for Christmas, which does not start with "x." Other notable examples were "ax," which does not start with "x," and "ox," which also does not start with "x".

Z

Zero-sum game: A mathematical representation in game theory where the net improvement of the total players is always zero and the gains of one player are exactly equal to the losses of another. This theory does not have to be visualized as various slices of pie being divided amongst a set group, but it usually is. Regardless of outcome it is impossible to increase the value of the participating groups' efforts from their initial value.

Works Cited

Your Mom: Volume I-IX (Published: Late stone age by Fat Whale Press. Author: unknown)

Passages: I took the lost points on every single school project I ever half-assed because I refused to make one of these stupid fucking things even when my academic future and potential lifetime earnings were at stake. What makes you think that I would willingly create a works cited page when it would have zero benefit to me other than validating my claims and legitimizing the facts that I am presenting to the audience, thereby giving me credibility and a level of professionalism expected in non-fiction work? The hell would be the point of that? Just do what I do when I am researching something and incorrectly type in your query to a search engine, let them autocorrect to the actual thing, and scroll down until you see something that mimics the beliefs and opinions you already have and use that. If you don't see anything like that, just scroll back up to the Wikipedia entry, take everything you read there as absolute fact and use whatever you read to fail to impress your crush the next time you see them... you know... like an adult.